More Praise for
The Secrets of Happy Families

"*The Secrets of Happy Families* is a gift! Family life today is so complicated, how could one book possibly sum up all the common factors? But Dr. Scott does it again. Incorporating important research, real-life stories based on an extensive survey, along with personal and professional experiences, this book can help anyone who is looking for keys to strengthen their family bonds. With a state-of-the-art 'positive psychology' approach, this book goes beyond the common sense that having a happier family comes from being constructive and loving; it provides many concrete, practical ways to get started immediately. And, for those who may be struggling but have the wish for a happy family, this book is full of gems that are presented in a clear and often touching way that is inspirational. *The Secrets of Happy Families* is one of those rare books that you can start anywhere, that you won't want to put down, and that you will want to keep close by."
> —**Rita DeMaria, Ph.D.,** coauthor, *The 7 Stages of Marriage*

"What's the secret to a successful family? A wise man once said the most important thing a father can do for his children is love their mother. Haltzman spells it out brilliantly and shows step-by-step how the parents' commitment and attachment—their marital bond—is the key to the successful family kingdom. Kids imitate what they see—they bond to the bond between the parents—and that secure attachment frees them to love, grow, play, thrive, and recover from whatever life throws them."
> —**Diane Sollee, MSW,** founder and director, Coalition for Marriage, Family and Couples Education (CMFCE), www.smartmarriages.com

"*The Secrets of Happy Families* is a well-researched and compelling guide for today's families. I highly recommend it!"
> —**Joshua Coleman, Ph.D.,** author, *When Parents Hurt: Compassionate Strategies When You and Your Grown Child Don't Get Along*

"*The Secrets of Happy Families* offers families a number of important and timeless lessons that we need to relearn. First, money doesn't buy families happiness. What does? Service to others, commitment to a family mission, unique family rituals and traditions, and a good measure of (mostly nonelectronic) family fun. Second, couples who acknowledge, appreciate, and work with—rather than fight against—the gender differences that characterize their relationship styles are more likely to enjoy their interactions with one another. Finally, and most importantly, Scott Haltzman reminds us that the foundation of any good relationship, and especially a strong family life, is commitment. Spouses, parents, and children thrive when they know that they will survive the inevitable ebbs and flows of family life and still have one another for the journey of life, come what may."

—**W. Bradford Wilcox, Ph.D.,** associate professor, Department of Sociology, University of Virginia; author, *Soft Patriarchs, New Men: How Christianity Shapes Fathers and Husbands*

"According to Dostoyevsky, 'Happy families are all alike.' In his recent book on the family, Scott Haltzman reveals their secrets. Based on clinical experience and research, the author provides all types of families with clear information and guidance on how to create a sustainable connection. This is a wonderful book. I recommend it to all families as required reading."

—**Harville Hendrix, Ph.D.,** author, *Getting the Love You Want* and *Giving the Love That Heals: A Guide for Parents*

"The secrets that Dr. Scott offers to create a happy family need to be revealed to all stepfamilies because their transition and normal development is challenging and takes a long time. Adults who consider remarriage with children need to read this book because any secrets, trail maps, workshops, books, or other guidelines are essential for building the complex stepfamily into a strong, successful one."

—**Elizabeth Einstein, LMFT,** cofounder, Stepfamily Association of America (now the National Stepfamily Resource Center); author, *Strengthening Your Stepfamily*

"This book is the natural progression from *Secrets of Happily Married Men* and *Secrets of Happily Married Women.* Dr. Haltzman's clear and engaging writing style reflects the range of his roles as a psychiatric clinician, researcher, astute observer, and family man. Based on wider definitions of 'family' and the potential complexity of current domestic households, this book embellishes the cited maxim 'Happiness is not a destination.' That trip, and the reader's course in the book, are guided by theories, many illustrative examples, and plenty of direct findings and recommendations. The humanity of the process is always central, and a gentle sense of humor is never too far away."

—**Chandran Kalyanam, M.D.,** assistant professor of clinical psychiatry, Ohio State University; author, *Seeking an Alliance: A Psychiatrist's Guide to the Indian Matrimonial Process*

"Reading this book is like listening to a wise and caring uncle—who also happens to be a terrific therapist. *The Secrets of Happy Families* is upbeat, grounded, and relevant to all kinds of today's families. Scott Haltzman has delivered again!"

—**William J. Doherty, Ph.D.,** professor of family social science, University of Minnesota; author, *Take Back Your Marriage*

The Secrets of Happy Families

Eight Keys to Building a Lifetime of
Connection and Contentment

Scott Haltzman, M.D.
with Theresa Foy DiGeronimo

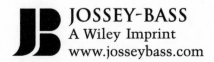

JOSSEY-BASS
A Wiley Imprint
www.josseybass.com

Copyright © 2009 by Scott Haltzman. All rights reserved.

Published by Jossey-Bass
A Wiley Imprint
989 Market Street, San Francisco, CA 94103-1741—www.josseybass.com

The anecdotes in this book are based on the life experience of the authors and the clinical work and research of Dr. Haltzman. To protect confidentiality, names and identifying characteristics of clients have been changed, or represent composite identities of clients.

Readers should be aware that Internet Web sites offered as citations and/or sources for further information may have changed or disappeared between the time this was written and when it is read.

Jossey-Bass books and products are available through most bookstores. To contact Jossey-Bass directly call our Customer Care Department within the U.S. at 800-956-7739, outside the U.S. at 317-572-3986, or fax 317-572-4002.

Jossey-Bass also publishes its books in a variety of electronic formats. Some content that appears in print may not be available in electronic books.

Library of Congress Cataloging-in-Publication Data

Haltzman, Scott, date.
  The secrets of happy families : eight keys to building a lifetime of connection and contentment / Scott Haltzman with Theresa Foy DiGeronimo.
       p. cm.
  Includes bibliographical references and index.
  ISBN 978-0-470-37710-9 (cloth)
  1. Family. 2. Family—Psychological aspects. I. DiGeronimo, Theresa Foy. II. Title.
  HQ734.H2565 2009
  646.7'8—dc22   2009001138

Printed in the United States of America
FIRST EDITION
HB Printing   10 9 8 7 6 5 4 3 2 1

Contents

To Susan, Matthew, and Alena
For all that you have taught me about family

Acknowledgments

Whenever I get my hands on a book, I flip to the acknowledgments page, just to see if there's a name there I'll recognize. Kind of like the credits at the end of the movie: just who was the key grip, anyway (and, as important, just what *is* a key grip)?

So to the readers who look over this page, recall that although these names may not be recognizable to you, they played a huge part in the formation of this book.

In order of appearance, thanks to:

Alan Rinzler, executive editor at Jossey-Bass, who came up to me after my presentation at an annual conference of the Coalition for Marriage, Family and Couples Education and said he wanted to be my publisher. Alan led the J-B team for *Secrets of Happily Married Men* and *Secrets of Happily Married Women*, and now for this new book, *Secrets of Happy Families*.

Susan Haltzman, my wife, who listened to my endless discourses about this book and watched helplessly, but lovingly, as I poured myself into my research and writing.

Theresa Foy DiGeronimo, who kept my writing in focus, and whose passion for the vitality of family life can be found in every page of this book.

Mary Codd of Growing Minds, Inc., who continuously reshaped my Web site, www.DrScott.com, to meet my research and marketing needs.

Betty Galligan of Newberry PR, for helping promote my work.

Christian Stephens, president and CEO of NRI Community Services, Nancy Paul, CEO of SSTAR, and Pat Emsellem, COO of SSTAR, for supporting my endeavors.

Jeannie Kim, deputy editor at *Redbook,* for believing in my message, and all the great *Redbook* readers who provided such useful information to me.

Sheena Berg at Blended-Families.com, for helping get the word out about the Happy Family Survey, thus prompting a flood of contributions. The chapter on blended families is born of her efforts.

Diane Sollee, founder and director of the Coalition for Marriage, Family and Couples Education (CMFCE) and editor of www.smartmarriages.com, for supporting my mission and for encouraging her readers to participate in the Happy Family Survey.

Christopher Chartier, who tirelessly and joyfully helped collect the survey data.

My father, Jay; my parents-in-law, Walter and Jane; and my siblings, Jonathan, Mark, and Jennifer, for their encouragement and interest in my work.

The staff at Jossey-Bass/Wiley, including Carol Hartland, Nana Twumasi, Jennifer Wenzel, Michele Jones, and Debra Hunter, who helped make this book a reality.

My clients, who never stop teaching me and who shared their stories with me.

The many individuals who took time out of their day to tell me about their families through the Happy Family Survey. Many of the comments that were sent to me were absolute jewels, but only a few could be used in this book. I'd like to thank everyone who participated. You've helped me treasure my family as never before.

The Secrets of
Happy Families

Introduction

It's about 11:30 P.M. My wife, Susan, and I are still awake, waiting to hear our seventeen-year-old daughter's car pull into the driveway. We had planned a calm evening; after all, Alena had called to tell us she was going to sleep over at a friend's house. Before the evening got too late, we tried to reach her on her cell phone, but she didn't answer. About five phone calls later to different households, and after another parent's drive around the block, we finally tracked our daughter down, at the house of another friend the next town over!

When Alena got on the phone, we barked, "Get home right this minute!" She put up a weak struggle, then agreed to come home. So, here we are now, prepared to talk to her about what happened and what we plan to do about it.

Is this the portrait of a happy family? By anyone's definition, the Haltzmans ought to be. We live in a small suburban town that, in 2005, was voted by *Money* magazine as one of America's ten best towns to live in. I earn a respectable income, and our home is solidly constructed. I have a wife of twenty-one years, two healthy and well-educated children, and a pet rabbit who is trained to go in one little corner of his cage. (We tried a dog once, but it didn't work out. That's another story.)

So if the Haltzmans fit such a perfect profile of a happy family, why are we all feeling so unhappy now?

That's the question I ponder as I sit down to write this book. What makes a happy family? Is it living in a good home? Making lots of money? Is it being warm, connected, trusted and trusting from cradle to grave? Must a happy home be conflict free, or can it include clashes and periods of discontent?

These aren't easy questions to answer for any of us.

ESSENTIAL FAMILY INGREDIENTS

As I attempt to reason through these questions, I find myself stuck on a key point: before I can answer questions about happy families, I first have to rethink my definition of *family*.

I've got a wife and two children, so just about anyone on the planet would agree that I'm part of a family. But mine isn't the only kind of family on this planet. Just last week, a client came into my office expressing real pleasure that I wrote a book called *The Secrets of Happily Married Women*, but she was a bit dismayed when she found out that the book focused solely on women's relationships with men. After all, she had been legally married to a woman for nearly two years and has now been trying to get pregnant through donor sperm. She wondered when I planned on writing a book for her.

Around the same time, I interviewed a client who, now a father himself, reflected back on his experience of being raised by his grandparents. When he celebrates Mother's Day, he sends a card to his grandmother. He still calls his mother every now and then, but feels no special connection to her. He and his grandparents were a family.

If there's any doubt that the definition of family is in flux, the point was brought home to me in late summer 2007 when I was invited to my son's college early in his freshman year. In years past, this special weekend event to check out your freshman's progress was called Parents Weekend. My weekend invitation, however, arrived with the following information:

*University College will host its annual
LSU Family Association Weekend, formerly
called 'Parents' Weekend.*

My theory about this change of wording: it just won't do, in this day and age, to assume that a family consists of two biological parents. Want a stat to back that up? According to the U.S. Census Bureau's 2004 *Household Economic Studies*, only 61 percent of children are raised from birth to age eighteen in a home with both of their birth parents.[1]

What this statistic tells us is that if we as a society don't open our eyes to new ways of defining family, we'll miss a real opportunity to make our families and our communities stronger. Throughout the pages of this book, you'll see that the secrets of happy families apply to all shapes, styles, and sizes—and certainly you!

This book will explore the many ways in which humans (and occasionally house pets) come together to form a family. But keep in mind that this book is about happy—not perfect—families. When I tell you that we were up past midnight talking to my daughter about the importance of letting us know where she goes, you know we've got potential problems. Everyone does. No family is perfect.

GETTING TO THE HEART OF REAL FAMILIES

As my wife and I dealt with our own family problems, I again wondered about this happy family idea. I have had a gut feeling for a long time that there is a difference in the happiness levels of families that join together in times of trouble to strengthen each of the individual members, and families that are so unwieldy that the members don't know from one day to the next where they are headed.

Although I'm a practicing clinician, I'm also a researcher, so when I have a gut feeling about something, the next step is to do some investigating to find out if it's true. I wanted to expand on my office-based experience and provide something concrete about families to share with you—something supported by data collected from all kinds of families from all over the country. So I created an online Happy Family Survey to help me gather hard numbers and real stories to back up the perspectives I've collected from hundreds of family members over the years.

The survey was advertised through various Web sites, including my own at DrScott.com and other Internet outlets, and it received mention in *Redbook* magazine. I distributed circulars to therapists in my community and at conferences, and I pitched my survey on several radio stations throughout the United States and Canada.

Word spread quickly, and between February 1 and December 5 of 2008, 1,266 family members completed the form.

I then sifted though mounds of data and used the information provided by the participants to gain a clearer understanding of the behind-the-scenes working of families. Because the participants were self-selected to take my survey, the results cannot be considered statistical proofs. (When possible, however, I matched my information against published data, and in almost every case, the statistics yielded in my survey matched national averages.) Yet the results have given me an open and honest look inside the heart of today's families.

SHARING REAL SECRETS

Psychiatrists are trained to hold closely to a code of confidentiality. When I invite people into my office, I find that they share with me experiences, insights, and events that have never been imparted to anyone else. It's the nature of the therapeutic process that when a person is given a venue to discuss his or her inner world, that person gains a new and better understanding of himself or herself.

Through my years of doing Internet research, I have found the same phenomenon. I was intrigued with how willingly those who participated in my online Happy Family Survey shared their family secrets under the cloak of Internet anonymity. Even the 2 percent of respondents who ranked "keeping family secrets" as a top priority filled out the survey!

Given an opportunity to "talk" online about their lives, their thoughts, and their passions, individuals freely shared family details. They shared information about roles in the household, from who initiates sex (men: 83 percent of the time) to who primarily buys relationship books (women: 65 percent of the time).

Beyond this kind of general information, people also willingly shared very personal experiences and insights that they had gathered over years of living as members of their families—things they would probably not reveal about themselves in general conversation. Some acknowledged that they were "extremely unhappy" in their family life and explained exactly what was missing in their relationships. Others wrote about the painful impact on the family of heartbreaking life events. All the respondents opened up their inner world and shared their secrets in the hopes that the readers of this book would reap the benefits.

The final results of this survey have shown me that there is no easy one-size-fits-all path to familial bliss. There is no Fam-o-Matic that will chop, slice, dice, and ripple-cut your way to happiness. But there are some fundamental things that you can do to get more of what you want from your life. Those who characterized their families as happy tended to agree that this state comes not from being the person with the most money on the block or by having the most trophies on the mantel, but by applying certain principles and behaviors that give them a sense of shared identity and commitment.

AN INVITATION

I'm hoping that by the end of this book, you will have an insider's understanding of how the secrets of other families can help your family. You will read the stories of others who have worked hard to establish identifiable family values, make a long-term and unbreakable commitment to each other, support each other through difficult times, expect and accept that kids change everything, work to find unity and common ground when they create a blended family, learn how to fight fair, bounce back when life gets tough, and take time to relax, enjoy, and breathe.

I now invite you to share in the secrets that can give you the kind of family life that you've always dreamed of.

Chapter 1

What Is a Family?

E very morning in homes across America, alarm clocks blare on bedside stands, showers fill with steam, and coffeemakers spew out fresh java. As the day passes, front doors open and shut, mail slots open and close, and dishes slowly pile up in sinks waiting once again to be washed and returned to cabinets. As the evening winds to a close, lights turn on and off, television channels flip, computers click and clack, and, finally, alarms are again poised to blare the next day.

While all the events of day-to-day life pass routinely from sunup to sundown in these houses and apartments across the land, it's the people within—the members of the family—who make these rooms a home for all who dwell there. We all know what we mean when we talk about family, but we may not all mean the same thing. What exactly is a family? Answering this question is my first challenge in writing this book. And I've learned that it's not as easy as I had first thought to clearly define this word.

In my years as a psychiatrist, I've evaluated thousands of individuals and spent countless hours interviewing hundreds of family members. By now, you would think, I'd have it all figured out. Well . . . actually . . . no, I don't. At least not that simply. Through the course of my clinical experience, one glaring truth emerges: no two families are the same. And certainly no two families function in exactly the same way. There's something both frightening and inspiring in that finding. Frightening because it means that as a psychiatrist and researcher of human behavior, I cannot apply one standard or formulaic set of techniques to my work with the many families who come to me for help. Inspiring because it demonstrates the diversity and breadth of experience, culture, and style that define the uniqueness of the word *family*.

FAMILY THROUGH THE AGES

Webster's *Third New International Dictionary* has twenty-seven entries for the word family.[1] The definition "a group of persons of common ancestry" is as clear and acceptable a definition as any, I suppose. But in her article "Family Versus Familia, Historical Definitions of the Family," Rachael Hughes reminds us that "our modern usage of the word family as a unit of relatives is relatively new." She explains further that the word grew from the Latin term *familia*, meaning "household," which included everyone—friends, relatives, servants, and slaves—living in that domicile.[2]

This is interesting stuff. It means there was a time when the word family did not apply to pesky in-laws who lived in their own household in another city, two days' wagon ride away. Or even to a beloved brother who established his own family two doors down. A little more research, and I found that it was not until the seventeenth and eighteenth centuries that family began to connote the intimacy of what we now call a nuclear family.

Before we move forward to discuss *happy* families in Chapter 2, I think there's something to be learned about our own families by taking an historical look at the family unit.

EVOLUTION OF THE FAMILY

A brief overview of family life through the ages makes it clear that one definition of family does not fit all. We could begin in the Garden of Eden with Adam and Eve and their sons Cain and Abel

SECRETS FROM RESEARCH
Family Buzzwords

These popular terms regarding the family were introduced to our language only over the last two hundred years or so:[3]

1796: in a family way (pregnant)
1809: family circle
1856: family man (one devoted to wife and children)
1966: family values

as our first family and find lies, betrayal, and murder—a rocky start to unity and happiness. In prehistoric times, the so-called family unit existed purely for survival purposes; during their short and brutish lives, the men were hunters and warriors who spent much of their time away from home and hearth, and the women bore children and died young. Jumping forward to the Middle Ages, in upper-class families, marriage was commonly a strategic arrangement to promote military, economic, or political goals. And then during the Industrial Revolution, factories lured fathers, mothers, and even children out of their homes with the promise of economic stability. The evolution of society and civilization has routinely changed the purpose, structure, and definition of the family.

I readily admit that I'm not an historian. I'm a shrink. But I find that diving into the history of the formations of families is critical for a good understanding of why and how families function. My search through the history books makes one thing glaringly clear: families adapt to and are defined by the culture that surrounds them. The meaning of family and the behavior expected within a family are very closely tied to their historical context.

This evolution of the family image continues even today. Many people challenge the notion that the family is composed of a husband

SECRETS FROM RESEARCH
Women in the Mosou Chinese Culture

What we might think of as the conventional male-headed household is not conventional for everybody. In the Mosou culture of Himalayan China, for example, women are considered leaders in the community, are granted special status when they reach thirteen years of age (as well as a house of their own), and can choose sexual mates at will. In this culture, when women give birth to a child, the father has no ownership of the child at all. As women grow in status, they pass on their power to other women, including the power to have or reject a man in their lives.

and wife with biological children, and perhaps a grandparent or two. Although this depiction certainly does fit the Merriam-Webster definition of "a group of persons of common ancestry," the twenty-first-century family is that and then some. An increasingly large proliferation of types, dynamics, and relationships based on sexuality, culture, religion, ethnicity, ideology, and other crucial variables can be seen all around us and is also quite evident in my own clinical practice.

THE MODERN FAMILY

The most recent and obvious shifts in today's modern family have occurred in the changing of gender roles within the family. In many families, the male is no longer the unquestioned head of the tribe—nor does he wish to be. He and his female partner more equitably divide the household roles—both taking greater responsibility for the care of the home and the children. Also, today both the male and female heads of the family may choose to work outside the home to earn a living, leaving the care of the children to caretakers who may or may not be related or members of the household.

Further, not all of today's families are bound by a common ancestry. Consider stepparents and stepchildren; adoptive parents and children; foster parents and children; childless married couples; unmarried but cohabiting couples; infertile couples with egg- and sperm-donor children; same-sex couples; same-sex couples and their adopted, foster, or egg- and sperm-donor children. Whew!

This extended view of the family begins to look more like the pre-seventeenth-century version of the family as "everyone living in the household," regardless of ancestry. So again, I face the dilemma of defining family before I can move on to Chapter 2!

SECRETS FROM RESEARCH
Commodore Perry's Unavailable Wife

In our society, monogamy between committed partners is considered an essential element in a happy family. But that's not the case in all cultures. Stories of early expeditions to the North Pole tell us that when Commodore Perry arrived with his wife to set up base camp in the Arctic, an Eskimo chief commented on how attractive Mrs. Perry was. Later, Perry was surprised to find that this chief was insulted when Perry thanked him for the compliment and continued his work. It turns out that in Eskimo culture, if someone compliments your wife, you're supposed to offer her up to have sex with the flatterer.[4]

Why do I suspect that this quaint idea will never catch on in twenty-first-century Western culture?

WHAT A FAMILY IS NOT

As I was writing *The Secrets of Happily Married Men* and *The Secrets of Happily Married Women*, I tried my best to include what I felt was a representative view of married couples. I made an effort to include stories of clients who weren't necessarily white or middle or upper class, but who instead were representative of a cross section of American life. I patted myself on the back, convinced that I had a broad worldview. Yet as I spent more time talking to my clients, meeting with trainees in psychiatry programs in New England, and traveling around the country giving lectures, an unsettling realization began to set in.

Whereas I thought I had taken an inclusive approach to discussing how to have a happy marriage, it was clear that there was a lot more to this "family" thing than I realized. Certainly, I can say without hesitation that many, many people experienced relationship issues very much like those I wrote of. There are male husbands and female wives who formally married and sought and found ways to balance home life and work life. Some are struggling to manage the care of children, some deal with in-laws, sex, money . . . all the things I had written about.

But just as often, people would approach me and ask why I didn't write about something other than the conventional cliché Norman Rockwell version of family. Here are some of the questions I fielded as I traveled the country:

> "Why don't you write a book about families who don't fit the traditional mold?"
>
> "Why don't you write about families that include a stepparent?"
>
> "Do you think you'll ever write books for people who just live together?"
>
> "How come when you write a book for happily married women, you assume they're married to men?"

"Can't my husband and I be considered a family even though we don't have any children?"

"I may be raising my children without a spouse, but don't we still count as a family?"

The more I talked to people from all walks of life, the less certain I became about how to define a family. One thing that did become glaringly clear to me was that I could not write a book about happy families by focusing only on the typical and traditional Western version of family. To do so would be to turn a blind eye to the many, many variants of the unit called family today.

So, thought I, perhaps I could begin to define a family by first defining what it is not. Surely it is now obvious that family *cannot* be defined strictly as comprising one biological father, one biological mother, and 2.4 children all lovingly going to church in their Buick on a Sunday morning in spring.

There. That's a start.

MOVE OVER, MRS. CLEAVER

Acknowledging that this stereotypical definition is no longer valid is, I suppose, an invitation for criticism. There is a concern in this country that the decline of the family institution embodied by the likes of Beaver, Wally, June, and Ward Cleaver is the direct result of our accepting attitude toward divorce, shared custody, cohabiting without a marriage license, single parenting, same-sex couples, and other new, "far-out" untraditional departures from old-fashioned conventions.

Certainly these changes in the family structure have caused societal, economic, and personal problems. But as our brief historical overview of the family has demonstrated, these types of big shifts have happened before, and a broader and more encompassing definition is simply another inevitable step for the ever-evolving family unit. We could not have expected time to stand still or to embrace the Cleaver family model as the only legitimate family structure forever.

So, realizing that I want this book to be useful for individuals in all types of families, I had hoped that I was ready to move on to Chapter 2. But . . . not so fast.

How do I address you, the reader? If I talk about "you, your mate, and your children," I stumble on the first and most challenging hurdle in this book. Why, you might ask, do I say "your mate" instead of "your spouse"? Do I assume that you are living with someone, rather than married? In fact, why do I mention a mate at all? Can't families have just one adult? Moreover, you might also inquire why I write "your children"; many families have no children, and others claim their house cat or guard dog as bona fide family members. And another thing (since I'm on the topic), why do I assume that you are the head of household at all? Couldn't I also have written "Your mom, your dad, and your siblings" to acknowledge the very real possibility that young adults may choose to read a book about creating a happy family?

My own online survey further added to the possibilities (and the confusion). When asking participants to choose a "family type," I offered these eight options:

1. Spouse (opposite sex)

2. Unmarried companion (opposite sex)

3. Same-sex romantic companion or spouse

4. Biological child(ren) of current spouse/companion

5. Stepchild(ren)

6. Foster child(ren)

7. Parent(s) or other family members

8. Pets

I thought that should cover it, but just in case, I also offered the option of "Other" with the opportunity for explanation. When the results came in, it was clear that I had missed many possible family types. Take a deep breath and consider these "other" options offered by my respondents who said that their family consisted of themselves and these other individuals who live together in their home:

- "My son's girlfriend and their daughter"

- "My fiancée of nine years"

- "My divorced husband who is living with me and my son"

- "My adult sister"

- "My sister, brother-in-law, and two nephews"

- "Adult biological children of former spouse"

- "My companion's daughter"

- "My registered domestic partner"

- "My ex-same-sex partner and her granddaughter"

- "My second husband, his two children, and my two children"

- "My college roommate–girlfriend"

- "My daughter and her 23-year-old boyfriend"

- "My husband, my three children, my husband's two children, and our eleven grandchildren, oops! almost forgot the dog"

Okay then! The American family certainly is an inclusive one. So which of the above is closest to who you are, dear reader?

THE TWENTY-FIRST-CENTURY FAMILY

Stepparents and children, single-parent households, communal families, remarried parents, adoptive families, and the like are just beginning to redefine the twenty-first-century family. The future promises more changes as, for example, same-sex couples are offered the right to legal marriages, and lesbians choose to be impregnated through artificial insemination with donor sperm. Also, open adoptions now expand the family to include the presence of both the birth parents and the adoptive parents in the child's daily life. Even some sperm and egg donors and traditional surrogates are now taking active roles in the lives of their offspring, adding even more possibilities to that elusive definition of family.

The seemingly complicated family roots of an acquaintance of mine will not be entirely uncommon in the future. This couple has two children conceived through advanced artificial reproductive technology. In their case, the wife's eggs were mixed with donor eggs and fertilized with a mix of the husband's sperm and donor sperm. A resulting embryo was implanted in a traditional surrogate, who carried the child to term and handed him over to the intended parents, who may or may not be the biological parents. That's certainly a new definition of family. And it's totally legitimate. These folks are absolutely and totally a family!

WHAT KIND OF FAMILY ARE YOU?

If you'd like to categorize your family type, you might fit into one of these (or you might not!):

Nuclear family: parents and one or more biological children. These parents may be married, may cohabit, or may be gay or lesbian.

Single-parent family: one parent and a child or children.

Extended family: a nuclear or single-parent family that lives with relatives outside the nuclear family, such as in-laws, grandparents, or adult siblings.

Blended family: a nuclear family in which one or both of the partners have children from a previous relationship; also a nuclear family that includes a foster child or adopted child in an open adoption.

Adoptive family: may be nuclear, single-parent, or blended. The child is not blood related to the parent, but has been adopted legally.

Foster family: can be nuclear, single-parent, or blended. One or more of the children are not birth or adopted children. The child may stay with the family for an extended period through an arrangement with special government agencies.

A.R.T. family: any family unit in which the children are the result of artificial reproductive technology involving the use of donor eggs or sperm, or a traditional surrogate.

Other family types: any group that does not consist of parent and children; for example, a newly married couple, same-sex couple, cohabiting couple.

In my research for this chapter, I've waded through what seemed like tons of information on the family, looking for that elusive descriptor that I feel can be applied to the diverse family landscape of the twenty-first century.

Coming up empty, I've decided to create my own definition. After much thought and reflection, I feel very comfortable defining family as "two or more people committed to sharing their life together who are related by blood, adoption, marriage or cohabitation, legal decree, or personal devotion."

That should cover it. Sure, some of the topics discussed in the following chapters will be of interest only to families headed by married couples, or only to families with children, or only to families of same-sex couples, or . . . well you get the idea. But remarkably, what I have discovered by researching the wildly diverse and eclectic groups called the American family is that those things that make family members happy are usually universal and true regardless of how families define themselves. No matter what the diverse configuration or sexual, cultural, ethnic identity, the basic ingredients of happiness in the family are pretty much the same, as you'll see once we get down to it in Chapter 2.

Chapter 2

What Is
Happiness?

Almost every day, a research paper or article comes to my attention reporting that increased work productivity, improved physical health, longer-lasting marriages, and overall sense of well-being all correlate with one factor: happiness.

Whether you've read these studies or not, I'm sure you've got a good sense that, all things being equal, it's better to be content than to be miserable. But seeking happiness and finding happiness don't always go hand in hand. I certainly hope that by reading this book and applying the lessons learned from other happy families, you are able to increase your own happiness. But before we talk about the "how," let's look at the "what."

FACTS ABOUT HAPPINESS

I believe that every human being has the potential to develop a solid, long-lasting core of happiness. Some spend a lifetime meditating, reading self-help books, or doing drugs in order to find a moment of happiness, but in doing so, they miss the point.

Happiness is not a final destination. It is a process, a journey, a by-product of a life well lived.

Only you can define exactly what happiness is for you and your family. And only you will know when you are feeling it. I, along with other folks who have kindly shared their insights on family

19

Secrets of Happy Families

Love the Ones You're With

I love my life! Happiness is about loving the ones you are with and loving them right, as well as loving them the way you want to be loved in return! Sure, I am like most others when it comes to money and such—always wanting more of that—but when it comes down to what truly matters in this world—love—I feel rich as they come!

—Roxanna, 32, married 8 years, with two children (husband adopted one of her children)

---

happiness in this book, can offer only guidance and advice based on our own experiences that we hope will help you find your way to your own happiness.

So let's begin by reviewing some facts from happiness researchers, who look past plastic surgery, fancy homes, and lots of money for the true source of happiness. Research points to specific concrete things that do in fact nurture internal, long-term happiness. That list includes the following:[1]

Religion. Involvement in faith improves social and community ties, which leads to greater happiness.

Sense of humor. People with a hopeful outlook that demonstrates joy to others are less likely to be dragged down by negative events.

Free time. Activities that combine socializing, physical activity, and the need for some level of skill are shown to lead to happiness.

Secrets of Happy Families

Happiness Is Somewhere in Between

Some people can never be happy unless the conditions are what they consider to be absolutely perfect. The job, the house, the money in the bank, their waistline, hairline, kids' school, you name it. They have to have all of the above to be happy at all. They think that some day when all this happens at once, they'll find true happiness. And they're always disappointed, whether they get it or not, since the list of requirements keeps getting longer.

Other people manage to find a little joy here and there—enough to keep them happy. They cherish and savor each one of these moments that might be overlooked by someone else. And they're always smiling like idiots—even though the rest of us can't see any reason to smile.

I try hard not to be the first type, and I wish very hard that I could be the second type. But with all the demands of life, I'm just happy to be somewhere in between.

—*Charles, 49, married 28 years*

Social skills. Friendship brings joy and opportunities for cooperation, sharing, and laughter.

Being cooperative. People who enjoy getting along with other people report higher levels of happiness.

Volunteering. "In one study, volunteer and charity work generated more joy than anything except dancing," reports *Psychology Today* writer Kathleen McGowan. "The sense of accomplishment, the social connection and the chance to do something meaningful are what make it so much fun."

Not coincidently, all these doors to happiness were mentioned by many who responded to my online Happy Family Survey. Surely there is something profound and consistent in them. According to Dr. Martin E. P. Seligman, the founder of positive psychology and one of the world's authorities on happiness, that's because each of these elements promotes the human characteristics that correlate with happiness: selflessness, gratitude, hope, zest, and the ability to love and be loved.[2]

SECRETS FROM RESEARCH
Happiness Is in Giving It Away

Money may not be able to buy happiness, but giving it away can lift your spirits. Research subjects were given money. Half were told to keep all of it; the other half were asked to give it away to a friend or a charity. Later in the evening, when the investigators asked the subjects about how happy they were in general, the ones who gave away money felt significantly happier. It's not receiving money but how you spend it that affects how good you feel.[3]

When we open all these doors, we experience the three factors that Seligman believes must all be present if we are to be happy:

1. A pleasant life full of pleasure, joy, and good times. It's easy for most of us to think of the elements that make up the pleasant life, and those things are, as your grandmother always said, not necessarily what money can buy. In fact, money in and of itself does nothing to improve your level of happiness. Research shows that if you're dirt poor, money does help improve your sense of well-being, but once an individual or family is out of poverty, increasing amounts of money do nothing to increase their happiness.[4]

When I ask families to think about pleasurable events in their lives, they often recollect moments of togetherness, such as the time that there was a blackout, and they played cards by candlelight, or the family camping trip when they all tipped over in the rowboat. Even those nights soaking in the hot tub can create very special family moments, according to a close friend of mine. You might think that this is a good example of money buying happiness, but my friend Russell insists that it's not the hot tub itself that he loves. "When I sit outside with my kids or my wife, there's no television and no telephone. It's a great chance to catch up without distraction." (Of course, the jets of hot water soothing his sore muscles are pretty nice too.)

Pleasure in life can be found in many activities, from singing together to playing video games together. If you're having fun, it's one important element to true happiness—but not the only one.

SECRETS FROM RESEARCH
Happiness Is Relative

In 1974, economist Richard Easterlin published a study that became known as the Easterlin paradox. He found that having more money (absolute income) did not necessarily lead to more life satisfaction. Instead, it set the bar of happiness a bit higher. Relative income (how much one earns compared to others), in contrast, had a direct correlation to satisfaction levels.[5]

Let's say you get a whopping raise in pay and buy a larger house and better car, but then find out that your brother or sister or friend or neighbor or colleague (it really doesn't matter who) got a bigger raise and a bigger house and a better car. In this relative circumstance, you're likely to feel *less* happy than you were before you got your raise. So much for money making you happy.

2. An engaged life, in which you lose yourself to some passion or activity. When you spend time doing something you love, doesn't time fly? People who let themselves be absorbed in their activities tend to be happier than those who remain detached and uninterested. Families who find a shared interest seem to connect, to engage each other in their pursuit of fun.

Finding a way to be with the family and to do engaging activities can be a challenge, though, because the thing you may love can be a real downer to your clan. An example: my wife and son love to shop for clothes; my daughter and I are of the "see what you want, buy it, get out of the store" breed. It's clear that being in the mall together is a potential source of unhappiness. To solve the problem, my wife and son go to Macy's, while I peruse the Apple store and my daughter meets up with a friend at the Uno Chicago Grill for one of those fresh-baked chocolate-chip cookies. Thus each of us is engaged, and when we meet later that day in the parking lot, our family happiness quotient is off the charts (until the credit card bill arrives, that is!).

Think about the times you've returned from the Fotomat store with hundreds of photos from your family vacation. When you sit around the dinner table absorbed in recollection, *that's* engagement, and it's one of the ways you build happiness as a family.

TOP SECRET Secrets of Happy Families

Talk and Sleep and Play Together

I've been divorced and widowed, a single parent for more than sixteen years, and now very happily married for eight years to my third husband. I know I can survive and thrive alone . . . I've done it. But Richard enhances my life so much by his insights, generosity, and thoughtfulness. There is a respect and a deep sense of liking the other that permeates everything. We have a mutual ability to make one another laugh and an inability to stay angry with each other for any length of time. And, thank goodness, we have the wisdom to cultivate this relationship by "running away" every three or four months to B&Bs where we can talk and sleep and play together.

Happiness as an individual is really an extension of this deep emotional satisfaction as Richard's wife. I try to nurture all my relationships, as a mother to four kids, a daughter to elderly parents, a sister to four siblings, and a friend to a variety of women I've met in all the stages of my life. They all enrich my life and give me insights and strength in different ways.

I don't think of happiness as a constant or as a guarantee in life. Richard and I have struggled with all sorts of problems. But it is the knowledge that despite all my flaws and failings he is with me for "the long haul" that ultimately makes me feel safe and at peace. Maybe that's a better way to put it . . . I don't have the constant happiness of a fairy tale but the overall contentment of being in a lifetime friendship.

—*Janet, age 54, married 8 years*

3. **A meaningful life.** A meaningful life may not have many high moments or blissful immersions, but it is packed with purpose.

Ah, if only sitting in the hot tub, absorbed in memories of the trip to Kokomo Bay, would be all we needed for complete happiness! Although the science of positive psychology says that the first two factors are necessary, this third leg on the stool of real happiness, finding meaning in your actions, is critical.

Are your actions focused only on the here and now, or are you able to think about the greater good when you consider how you relate to the world? In the pages of this book, you'll read about the Gemma family, who initiated a national campaign to fight breast cancer after the death of their matriarch; you'll meet Sarah and Bill, whose children donated instruments to the Mr. Holland's Opus foundation; and you'll hear about Jan and her husband, who over the years have provided a foster home for boys in need. One common theme threads through these stories: these people are layering their life with meaning, with an eye toward doing things that matter, not just to them, but to the world as a whole.

Many families don't have the resources to develop a charitable foundation or raise a foster child, but every family can do things that leave a lasting impact on the world. Taking the family for a day of picking up garbage from the beach (usually on Earth Day) or going through the pantry for items to contribute when the Cub Scouts come by to collect food for the needy are just two examples of fun activities that, because of their contribution to the greater good, lead to happiness.

SECRETS FROM RESEARCH
Source of Joy

Happiness hides in the most interesting places. Dr. Nansook Park, a coauthor with Dr. Seligman, tells us that expressing gratitude to another person can actually make us happier. Here's how: "Gratitude boosts the morale of the person who receives it," Park explains. "That person tries to do better, and your relationship with him or her becomes stronger and you both feel happier."[6]

HAPPINESS THAT DOESN'T WAVER

What all this tells us is that when psychologists talk about happiness, they don't generally mean that heady feeling one gets after winning fifty bucks on a lottery ticket, or the satisfaction one feels when the home team comes in first again, or even the joy of an exhilarating run on the ski slope. They define it as *a sense of deep contentment*. That is the definition on which this book rests.

Yes, happy families have their moments of exhilaration, satisfaction, and joy, but they also are bound to have times of anger, sorrow, and despair. The factor that bolsters the good times and still defines a family as happy in the bad times is that feeling of deep contentment that transcends the momentary pleasures and pains. It does not waver based on the size of the home or the quality of TV reception or the cost of one's vacation.

Instead, contentment is something that grows over time, draws its strength from small day-to-day events and decisions, and plants its roots in activities that give our days meaning and purpose—without a conscious desire to own happiness. This view of happiness reminds me of the beliefs of John Stuart Mill, a nineteenth-century English philosopher: "Ask yourself whether you are happy, and you cease to be so. The only chance is to treat, not happiness, but some end external to it, as the purpose of life."[7]

In this book, I'll help you create the habit of focusing on the most important of those "external" forces, your family, by learning from the secrets of other happy families.

By proactively shaping the family life you desire, that life can be yours. Read on.

Secret 1

Happy Families . . .
Stick Together

"Hey Mom. That sign says kids under twelve get in for free. They won't know I'm really thirteen. Tell 'em I'm twelve, and you can save twenty-five bucks!"

Interesting observation. As a teenager, Jared already knows how to work the system. But even more interesting will be how his mother responds. What she does here will teach him a lot about his family's values—*if* the family has identified those values and agreed to practice them.

It's easy for me to sit at my keyboard and theorize on the proper response to Jared's proposal. But when we are faced with real-life situations, these kinds of decisions aren't so clear-cut. I've taken weeklong trips to all-inclusive resorts with my family, where the cost difference between taking along a twelve-year-old as opposed to a thirteen-year-old is hundreds of dollars. What would *you* do?

Certainly, it's the rare family member who would say out loud, "Good thinking, Jared. Because our family values saving money over honesty, we definitely should lie about your age to save a few dollars." It's more likely that Mom might say, "Jared! You know we've always taught you not to lie . . . But this *is* so expensive, so . . ."

Unless your family has consciously thought about its values and has agreed to make family decisions based strictly on those considerations, it's hard to know how to react when suddenly confronted with a situation like this one. It's quite likely that in a scenario like this, many moms, dads, brothers, sisters, grandmas, and grandpas would agree to compromise their alleged standards of truthfulness and pocket the money without dwelling on what this action says about the values ultimately upheld by the family.

A contradiction between what a family says about its beliefs and what it does on a day-to-day basis has the potential to cause friction that can wear away at happiness. In contrast, families who keep a clear view of what matters and live consistently by those values grow stronger over time. But, as Jared's parents and the vacationing Haltzmans can attest, sometimes living by what we believe isn't as simple as it looks.

DEFINING FAMILY VALUES

Sure, we all believe in family values, and we know that as a unit, our family has a unique identity based on our values. But have you ever stopped to think about how those values are chosen and developed? You do have a choice here: they can be actively molded with conscious effort, or they can be passively spawned in a haphazard way. I believe that family members tend to be happier if they make a conscious effort to know who they are, what they value—and why.

Secrets of Happy Families

It's Not About the Stuff

Making money and having "stuff" seems to be the end-all today. But unless you are truly connected to your partner and family, all the stuff in the world won't make a good family.

—*Elaine, 67, married 40 years*

Values Are Unique and Personal

Unfortunately, the expression *family values* has taken on a political connotation, as moral conservatives wave the family values flag, and liberals fear that the term is a catch-all intended to condemn any family that doesn't consist of a husband, wife, and 2.4 kids behind a white picket fence. But the true meaning and value of knowing what your family stands for have nothing to do with politics and everything to do with you and your unique family unit, whatever form, shape, or configuration that might be. I've heard from many people who consider their cats or dogs to be members of their families—and if that's your situation, your value system probably has a lot to do with them too.

Your family—not the president, not Congress, not your neighbors, not your boss, not anyone but you—gets to decide what your values are. And once you consciously make those decisions, your values are your guide to building a happy and resilient family. They will help you make decisions about everything from where to send your kids to school to whether you'll buy a new car, from where (or if) you go on vacation to whether you'll go to church. Even from whether or not you'll use creative accounting on your tax return to whether or not you'll tell the cashier she gave you too much change.

Your unique vision allows you to make life decisions that contribute to your family's happiness regardless of what the Joneses are doing. This is the key reason why families are all so different: we value different things. If, for example, one family believes that spending leisurely time together on family vacations is a priority, their lifestyle may confuse the family that places a higher value on financial security and wonders, "I just don't understand how the McCarthys can spend so much money on a vacation when they have two children who will be needing money for college in two years."

Spending money on things that the family considers high priority is neither right nor wrong; it is an expression of that family's values. And ultimately families need to accept the choices they make based on those values. When both parents consciously agree that family time together while raising their children is more important than saving for the expensive cost of highly selective universities, they will feel comfortable accepting the fact that their children will attend more affordable colleges, or they will take out loans to attend more expensive colleges. And everybody agrees to take the consequences of that decision.

Everybody in the McCarthy family is happy because the McCarthy Executive Parenting Team has agreed on the value of family vacations. The children know that's how the process goes, and that's the beauty of family values.

Defining Your Values

This very first "secret" of a happy family isn't about my telling you what your family values should be. It's about sharing what some happy families say has worked for them, and helping you prioritize your own family values. It's about making yourself think about what brought you together as a family, whether it was marriage, adoption, or that night ten years ago when you needed a place to stay and ended up finding the love of your life. I want to help you uncover the core values that help keep you together and define your family identity.

It would be disingenuous to say that one value system is just as good as another. If you'd rather pay for Gucci shoes instead of a car seat for your young child, it would be pretty difficult for me to say, "That's okay! Who am I to judge?" Such a choice would be dangerous and amounts to potential abuse. But judgment aside, knowing what you honestly value can help you decide how you'll make decisions that keep the family safe and happy (even when you'd personally rather have the Gucci shoes!).

The word "value" is bandied about these days every which way. In the supermarket or on commercials, "value" is used to claim that the product or service being sold is worth more than you actually pay for it. Getting a dozen doughnuts for fifty cents would be a good value; getting a dozen grains of sand for the same price would not. Likewise, when a lesson or a jewel is valuable, it means that it has great worth, although, unlike the supermarket use of the word, it doesn't necessarily mean that you got it for a good price. When one person values a friend or mentor, he or she appreciates the qualities of that person.

When it comes to your family identity, *values* refer to an enduring system of beliefs that serves to steer the course of your life choices. Buying doughnuts, for instance, even at a good price, would not be considered a pervasive family value (unless you're Homer Simpson), but providing safe and healthy food for your family might be. Many vegans and vegetarians routinely make hundreds of decisions daily based on this belief system—for some it is a predominant influence in how they live their lives.

If you think of values this way, you'll notice that they are not fleeting or situation dependent; they are enduring, and they apply across a full range of activities and situations. Owning a flat-screen television is not a value. Choosing to support public television and watch educational programming together as a family is. Going to the weekend soccer tournament is not a value. Being near your children as they achieve in sports and academic pursuits is. See how it works?

Conflicting Values

Looking at values this way makes it tempting to sigh with relief, thinking "That was easy!" Yeah, if only! You see, the problem with values is that they frequently conflict with each other. For instance, if I asked you, "Do you value time with your family?" you'd probably say, "Of course." If I then asked, "Do you value the financial security that accompanies advancement at work?" most likely you'd say, "Yes." So what happens when your boss invites you to a weekend sales meeting, but your daughter has a swim meet? Or your parents are having their annual family picnic on the same day that your company is having "family day" and you, your husband, and kids are expected to be there? Two important values, but one has to trump the other.

Several years ago, I was interviewed by *Time* magazine for an article called "Stress and the Superdad," based in part on research done by *Spike TV*, which reported:[1]

> When asked to choose how they measure success, only 3 percent of men said through their work, while 31 percent said they did so through their faith in God, 26 percent through being the best person possible, 22 percent through their network of family and friends, and 17 percent through maintaining a balance between home and work.

Pretty convincing evidence that many men seem to have their values straight, isn't it? But the article goes on to point out some pretty disturbing realities:

> Despite their best intentions, however, men are not necessarily curtailing their work hours. Nearly 68 percent of men work more than 40 hours a week, and 62 percent are working on weekends. And men with children are putting in more hours than those without: 60 percent of them work 41 to 59 hours a week, whereas only 49 percent of men without kids rack up that many hours.

Engaging in an activity that results in the satisfaction of one value often comes at the cost of another. This is particularly true when members of a family disagree about the choice of values. After all, we each come from a family that had its own values (which we may want to keep or rebel against), and then when we build our own new family with another person, we must find a way to unify the value systems from both backgrounds. Not always easy.

Take Tatiana's situation, for example. Tatiana is a hard-working lawyer who is also sensitive and polite and in general an all-around good wife to her husband, Zach. Tatiana met Zach at work in a Dallas corporate headquarters; she worked in contracts; he worked in property appraisals. After a whirlwind romance, they decided to tie the knot. "I thought we shared the same values," Tatiana told me. "We talked about kids, politics, lifestyle. It was a match!"

Soon after the wedding, she went to visit her in-laws in their rural home. "It was the weirdest thing," she said. "All they wanted to do was sit in the den and watch TV. They never went out; they never spoke about anything that went on in the world. They just sat together staring at the TV screen." After spending the good part of the Memorial Day weekend watching TV in silence, Tatiana decided to go for a walk. She invited her in-laws and her husband to join her. They seemed confused ("Why would you want to go out for a walk?"), but according to Tatiana, it was either that or die from cabin fever, because Tatiana is the kind of person who really enjoys new things and adventures and fresh air!

Tatiana was learning that Zach's family value was togetherness and staying at home, which seemed endearing when Zach wanted to stay at home with her in their apartment rather than go out. But she didn't realize that it was what he *always* wanted to do. Therefore, as she and Zach build their own family, they will have to face this clash of values (and the others that will inevitably come along) and create their own set of accommodations, compromises, and sacrifices that meet both their needs. When and if kids come along, they'll learn to rethink their values again. This is an ongoing process, which never really ends.

As you read through this chapter, you'll be asked to consider what really counts in your life. The odds are that there will be a whole host of things about which you'll say, "Yeah, that's important." Once you have defined the things that matter to you, you've can go the next step and figure out how to prioritize those things for you and the other members of your family.

HAPPY FAMILY SURVEY

To create my online Happy Family Survey, I identified twenty specific values that many experts believe encompass basic human needs and wants. Respondents were asked to rank only three of these values as first, second, and third in importance. Folks could also answer "other" and provide important values of their own.

The following is that same list of twenty values. Please indicate which you believe are the top three values held by your family.

	Most Important	Second Most Importance	Third Most Importance
Financial security	_____	_____	_____
Health	_____	_____	_____
Protecting family secrets	_____	_____	_____
Formal education	_____	_____	_____
Personal and emotional growth	_____	_____	_____
Learning	_____	_____	_____
Personal appearance	_____	_____	_____
Serenity	_____	_____	_____
Comfort at home	_____	_____	_____
Generosity	_____	_____	_____
Justice	_____	_____	_____
Friends	_____	_____	_____
Elegance	_____	_____	_____
Contribution to society	_____	_____	_____
Spiritual fulfillment	_____	_____	_____
Work or employment	_____	_____	_____
Diversity	_____	_____	_____
Travel	_____	_____	_____
Fame	_____	_____	_____
Material possessions	_____	_____	_____

Perhaps you'd like to add other values to your top three. Several survey respondents added their own, including the following:

Self-respect	Safety
Honesty	Making contribution to society
Love	Family time
Integrity	Fidelity/faithfulness
Commitment	Fun
Openness	

So feel free to individualize!

THE RANKINGS, PLEASE!

Okay. Now put your own answers aside for a few moments while we look at how those who participated in the online survey ranked these values.

Certainly, the results of this kind of exploration vary from one family to the next. When I reviewed the data from all the completed surveys, virtually no two respondents ranked three of these twenty values in exactly the same way. However, there were some commonalities. For example, nearly half of all the respondents ranked "personal growth" in the top three, and only six people ranked "elegance" at all. When asked to prioritize values held by the family, the following five received the most votes (you can see the entire survey in the Appendix). I list them in the order in which they were most commonly endorsed.

1. Personal and emotional growth

2. Comfort at home

3. Health

4. Spiritual fulfillment

5. Financial security

To rank the given values, every one of the respondents had to ask himself or herself questions about how the family is structured around beliefs, traditions and principles, morals and ideals. We all need to do this to identify the values on which we want to build our families. So let's take a look at these five to see how they fit as family values.

Personal and Emotional Growth

In the book *Surely You're Joking, Mr. Feynman*, physicist Richard P. Feynman writes of his early childhood. He discusses living in Rockaway, New York, and of being fascinated with electronics. He would take radios apart and put them back together. After just a few years of playing around, Richard got quite a reputation for fixing radios and actually brought in a small income to his Depression-era home.[2] Nowhere in the book did he address what it must have been like for his family to have electronic equipment scattered about the house night and day. Maybe they liked the mess; maybe they didn't. But it's my best guess that they valued his inquisitive explorations that led to his intellectual and personal growth, not to mention a few more dollars coming in at a time when they really needed the money. I have no doubt that his family's appreciation of his need to tinker and repair provided a rich environment for mental growth that led ultimately to his helping develop the atom bomb and to receiving the Nobel prize for physics in 1965.

However, as we saw earlier in this chapter, sometimes values can conflict with each other. In choosing those we place at the top of our list, we must sometimes let go of others. For example, if a family places the value of order and cleanliness over personal growth, the members are unlikely to encourage the inquisitive mind that makes a mess with random electronic parts collected from all over the neighborhood.

Consider the story *Into the Wild*, in which journalist Jon Krackauer chronicles the last adventure of young college grad Chris McCandless (which was later brought to the silver screen by director Sean Penn).

With passion and a single-minded seriousness of purpose, McCandless sought to free himself of the encumbrances of modern life and to live off the earth. He is quoted as saying, "The core of man's spirit comes from new experiences." I don't think I'd be giving away too much of the plot when I reveal that almost two years into his quest, his frozen and emaciated body was discovered on an abandoned bus in the Alaskan wilderness. If his family valued self-exploration and growth, we can see that their grief would be tempered by an understanding of Chris's drive. But if personal safety was a higher value for them, their grief at their son's death would be unbearable. Values shape our view of life and love.

Comfort at Home

The ways one can attain comfort at home certainly vary from one home to the next. But generally, this value puts home life ahead of things like travel, socializing, and even personal growth. This is a value that helps you make the decision to beautify the backyard and deck, to add an addition, to redecorate, to focus on, well, being comfortable at home.

Marsha and Seth have put comfort at home at the top of their list. Here's why: Marsha is a successful investment banker from Providence, Rhode Island. Although she and her husband, Seth, would very much like to be parents, after twelve years of marriage, they haven't been able to conceive a child. As a childless family, their values are going to be different in some ways than those of other families. Neither of them puts a high priority on exotic or lengthy vacations; they go to synagogue on the High Holidays, but religion is not central to their lives. So what do they value?

This is a subject that they have talked about over the years, and as natural homebodies, they have agreed to put money and effort into establishing a warm home that is their retreat from the world. "But," says Seth, "it never felt just right until recently—after we added the final touch to make our home our castle." Now that Marsha has been made a partner in her firm, she is able to afford her dream: in the basement of their Victorian home, she and Seth have built a home theater complete with very comfortable reclining chairs, surround sound, and, of course, the five-hundred-inch screen. (I might be exaggerating on the screen size, but it *is* humongous.) Marsha and Seth entertain friends there, and frequently sit together and screen new movies. Marsha beams when she talks about her basement entertainment center and how much Seth enjoyed picking out the special screen and state-of-the-art projector. In a bizarre twist on the famous quote from *Jerry McGuire*, she says, "It completes us!"

And, hey, why not?

Health

For some people, health considerations are predominant concerns, and this fact affects how the family manages many aspects of their lives.

Logan is a good example of a man who places his health, and the health of his family, at the top of his list of priorities. Logan isn't a rich man. Because of his chronic depression, he receives Social Security disability payments, and he, his wife, and his two-year-old son get welfare and food stamps as well. They live in a small apartment. They don't have cable or fancy cell phones, and they wear sweaters to bundle up against the New England cold rather than spend a lot of money on utilities.

But when it comes to the health of his family, Logan spares no expense. He and his wife go to the high-quality, high-end supermarket, where they buy pure, organic foods at prices that are often twice as high as they might be in a conventional store. Logan says, "I know we don't have a whole lot of money, but I realize that the health of my child and my wife are in the balance. Buying healthy food is the best investment I know of."

Neighbors may be surprised to find Logan using his food stamps to buy top-dollar organic foods, but what *they* think doesn't matter. Logan puts health on the top of his family value list and is willing to sacrifice in other areas to stay true to that decision.

Of course, you might say, everyone values health. When expectant parents are asked what gender they would like their child to be, you know the answer: "It doesn't matter, so long as the baby is healthy." Still, even though health is a desired condition in life, not everyone puts it up as high on their family value list as Logan. If they did, surely they would work hard to always promote healthy habits, which can rule out raising kids on cheap, easy-to-grab-and-run nitrate-filled hotdogs and sugar-laden candy bars. This is a personal family choice that we all face.

Let's take the bicycle helmet debate, for example. If you have kids over the age of five who ride bicycles, you've had this debate. In our house, we value our health, and we insisted that our kids wear bicycle helmets. (No! not when they were just sitting around the house, but when they rode bicycles.) Once they hit about age twelve, many of their friends were allowed to ride without helmets. They also wanted to ride bareheaded. So we were stuck. If we valued their health over their fitting in with their peer group, then we would forbid them to go out without headgear. But if we put a premium on socializing and connection with others, then we'd take our chances and allow them to ride without helmets. Demanding head protection was not an easy decision, but it was made much easier for us because we had already decided to make family health a high priority.

Once the decision was made, I wasn't giving in. (I actually worked alongside a neurologist once who was no longer a practicing doctor because of a head injury he suffered while riding on a bicycle—without a helmet!) I do have to add that our teenage kids did not have exactly the same set of values as their parents, so they refused to ride their bikes at all once they encountered this Executive Parenting Team family rule.

Spiritual Fulfillment

Lots of families believe in God or a Higher Power. Lots of families go to church. But that doesn't mean that they hold spiritual fulfillment as a high-priority value. Spiritual fulfillment isn't just about what you do; it's about how you and your family members see the world.

Craig, for example, is a guy whose life mirrors his spiritual beliefs. He is a marriage mentor whose focus is on how to understand the effect of values on relationships. I got to know Craig and his wife, Susan, because I shared an exhibitor's table with them at a national marriage conference. (The conference, by the way, is called Smart Marriages, and if you ever get a chance to go, do it!) They practice the Baha'i faith, and their faith was indeed tested when, just two weeks after we all sat together at our table, Craig was diagnosed with a malignant brain tumor.

When I e-mailed him, I simply said, "Quite an ordeal that you have been dealing with, and I'm sure you've taken it on with great fortitude." To which he responded, "Thanks Scott. . . . It's really been much more of a spiritual journey than an ordeal."

Craig didn't have to think about that one. His spirituality drives his view of the world, even his view of his illness and the impact it has on him.

Even without organized religion behind their beliefs and values, many people give high priority to spiritual fulfillment. Ben is such a person. Ben is a client of mine whom I worked with during a period of time when he moved from his business job back into his home as a househusband. This forty-year-old businessman grew up in a middle-class, Jewish household in a New England suburb, so I was surprised to learn that after finishing college, he went off to Europe to spend three years learning transcendental meditation. He then went on to teach the discipline to hundreds of young men and women in the early 1970s, before going back into the world of corporate America.

It was a desire to find his core center again that pushed him to leave his corporate job and return home to give full attention to domestic duties. I found myself imagining what that must have been like, to make such a shift away from mainstream society in an effort to become more attuned to one's spiritual self. Ben told me that being very clear about what he valued made it easy for him to give up a life that didn't support the things he viewed as his life priorities.

Many of us recognize spirituality as a core component of our families. Several respondents to the online survey made that very clear and offered these insights:

> "Faith is an important foundation and hopefully parents teach through their example that a strong faith will enhance their entire lives."

> "God wrote the original rule book for families. If we will faithfully apply His principles both proactively and reactively we will succeed."

> "Religion is most important in my family. Even if all of us don't get along with each other, we all have the same foundation in our faith."

> "Faith helps everything else fall into place, no matter how many problems there are."

If spirituality (whatever that means to you) is one of your priorities, it certainly is a value that has the power to guide your family decisions and to lay a foundation for your family's identity.

Financial Security

My grandparents lived through the Depression, so my parents were raised to do everything in their power to make sure that the family kept afloat financially. My father went to Lehigh University on a partial scholarship, he lived at home, and in the evenings and weekends he drove an ice-cream truck. When he married, he joined the Air Force and was often away from his home. On the rare occasions when he and my mother went out to eat, they would go to an all-you-can-eat restaurant with my mother's purse lined with foil so that she could throw in a few pieces of fried chicken for the next day's lunch. After he left the service, my father worked a lot of hours managing his own paint and wallpaper store. After many years, he expanded to a total of three stores in three different cities. My mother began her own dance school, and, like my father, started three branches throughout their community.

I have no doubt that my parents managed to get by, raise a family, and stay together because of their shared values. Although I've never directly asked, "So Mom and Dad, in your early years together, what was your top family value?" I'm quite sure my father didn't live at home during college just because he valued tight family bonding (although he loved his family very much); I don't think my parents stashed away chicken because they valued stealing (*Is it really stealing if we paid for all we could eat?* they would rationalize); I don't think that my father spent time away from his family because

SECRETS FROM RESEARCH
The Price of Financial Security

It's a rare person who doesn't feel that financial security is important for a family. Of the 1,266 respondents to my Happy Family Survey, 30 percent listed financial security among their top three values. But, if you'll excuse the pun, valuing financial security comes with a price.

Social scientists have discovered a curious phenomenon. With the birth of a child, men work longer hours than before: 13 percent longer hours if it's a girl and 30 percent longer hours if it's a boy.[3] One could hypothesize that this extra work effort is simply an attempt on the man's part to get out of the house more, but I know, and you know, that that's not the case. Here's a great example of how seeking financial security conflicts with the value of family time. These new dads certainly want to spend time with their families, but feel compelled to spend time away from the home in order to provide for them financially.

he valued independence; I don't think that he worked that hard because he treasured fancy clothes or fast cars.

It is clear to me that my father and mother valued financial security, and they devoted the first twenty-five years of their life to establishing that for their family. Their plan worked, and as I grew up in that family, I never saw my mom line her purse with foil again (although my grandmother continued to snatch a few Sweet'n Low packages whenever we went to a restaurant).

SET YOUR VALUES

I find it interesting to examine what respondents to my survey do *not* value. Here are some interesting numbers out of the 1,266 total respondents:

- 15: The number who place **material possessions** among their top three family values

- 9: The number who place **fame** among their top three family values

- 6: The number who place **elegance** among their top three family values

- 19: The number who place **personal appearance** among their top three family values

Most individuals said that things like health, safety, family closeness, and spirituality were more important than fame and material possessions. If these results are representative of many families, then why do many families spend so much time and money on the pursuit of low-value things, even when they take energy and effort away from the family's high-end values? And, after investing untold time and money in pursuit of these less important things, why do families let them cause a disproportionate amount of family upset and even destruction?

Could it be because they're writing down answers they think will be socially acceptable and make them look good to whoever is compiling the survey? Maybe. I try to factor that in when interpreting this kind of self-test. But I think it's more likely to be because families who argue over these "unimportant" things haven't yet sat down to identify them as low-priority items in the grand scheme of things.

Time to Determine Your Family Values

It's time to get your family involved in choosing the values on which you'll build the family's happiness. To begin, gather together all family members who are old enough to understand the importance of having values. Usually once children are in school, they are ready to participate in the exercise (although they may get a bit fidgety after a while). Share the survey list and offer your top three choices. Then ask everyone to respond to your list and to make a list with their own top three. Don't debate or censor at this point; just jot down ideas that are prompted from the survey list or from your own beliefs and feelings. Remember, in this discussion there is no right or wrong; every family member should feel comfortable expressing the things that matter most to him or her personally (even when your teenager says that her principal value is to have her entire body covered with tattoos).

After this freewheeling sharing, it's time to make decisions about those values that the family as a whole feels are most important. As we will see, in households with children, this requires parents to balance adult-oriented needs (such as earning enough money to pay the rent) with the values of a younger generation (such as traveling the world together in a Winnebago). Ultimately, these top values will become part of your family's mission statement and will be used to make important family decisions.

Your values might, for example, support your decision to add an extension onto your home and forgo a family vacation if comfort at home trumps travel. Or, as in the McCarthys' case earlier in the chapter, it makes sense that they would prefer vacation time to expensive college educations for the kids because they have consciously placed travel and family together time over education. These kinds of decisions will be easier to make without argument or angst when you have your family mission statement to support the final choice. So choose your values carefully.

Keeping the list to a max of five is usually a good idea; any more than that becomes too hard to remember and focus on. This will be tough, because as you make your list you're bound to say, "That's important!" and "We need that too." You've designed a menu for yourselves, and there are lots of appetizing and healthy entrees to choose from. But it's not practical to choose everything on a menu, and for the sake of your family, you can't choose to have every value in action at the same time. This doesn't mean that if spiritual growth is ranked sixth on your list, it's not a family value at all. Of course it is, but its role in guiding the direction of your family's happiness is not as powerful as those values that come before it.

Dealing with Disagreement

Choosing your top values gets especially sticky when there's little agreement among family members about what's most important. When choosing her family's top three values, one survey respondent noted, "This is hard to answer because my husband's values are totally opposite of mine." And another: "This is definitely not MY top three, but this is what the majority in my household believes." Don't worry if that happens; it's natural. Identifying and resolving these differences can help you avoid a source of potential trouble down the line. You may be concerned about your children hijacking the proceedings and rallying together to vote for a trip to Disney World instead of going to junior high school. But remember, you're a charter member of the Executive Management Team, and you get to make the rules of this proceeding. Later on, we'll discuss ways to approach discussions to make sure that everyone is satisfied and reason prevails.

Frequently people don't realize that they do agree on many things, because they tend to focus on differences (we'll talk more about this in Secret 5). However, they actually agree on the general idea, and the disagreements are usually about the smaller details. For example, we might not agree on how much to spend on the new couch, but we do agree that we don't want to get in debt. Or we might not agree on what kind of dog to get, but we do agree that we want a pet. Or we might not agree on the style of home to buy, but we do agree that living in the country is preferable to living in a big city.

So when you open the discussion about choosing the important values, don't assume "we don't agree on *anything*!" Most likely, that's nonsense. There probably are lots of pockets of mutual agreement on routine things that give you common ground for finding points of agreement on value issues.

The Family Values Matrix

I want to introduce you to a very powerful tool that I use with my clients; it's a way to help you make sense of many needs that your family has defined. It's called the Family Values Matrix. I'll show you how to design the matrix for your family and use the results to help open up discussion and decide on the three to five values that best define your family.

To begin, take out the lists that each member of your family has compiled and ask each person to reveal his or her own top three. No debating or arguing at this point. Freestyle brainstorming is the goal. In fact, during this process, I suggest you set these ground rules:

1. Set aside family time for this important discussion.

2. Treat each member of the family with respect.

3. Be open to talking about all points of view.

4. Use the discussion as a chance to learn, not judge.

Now that we've all agreed to play fair and have some fun while we're at it, let's take a look at how the list is used. We'll take, for example, the Wray family, consisting of two parents and one daughter. Here's how their list is shaping up:

Basjana (Mom):   Generosity
                        Spiritual growth
                        Education

Jay (Dad):   Education
                        Comfort at home
                        Financial stability

Kristin (age 13):   Friends
                        Comfort at home
                        Travel

One thing that you'll notice is that Jay and Kristin both named comfort at home, and Basjana and Jay both said education. There's a good chance that this overlap of values will happen with your family as well. These shared values gain more weight later on.

Now it's time to see how these values match up against each other. This is not to say that one person's choices are better than another's, but identifying *family* values requires some give and take of personal beliefs so that you can come up with a list of three to five values that all family members agree will guide family decisions. Although the other values remain very important, occasionally they may need to take a backseat if they conflict with those you've given higher priority.

Across the top of a sheet of paper, write each of the values generated by the list. When a value is chosen more than once, write it only once, but note how many times it was chosen. In the case of the Wrays, the top of the matrix will look like this:

Generosity	Travel	Education (2)	Spiritual Growth	Comfort at Home (2)	Friends	Financial Security

Now list these exact same values vertically down the side of the paper. When you're done, you will have a chart that lists your family's choices. It will look something like the Wray's chart, although yours may be smaller or larger depending on the number of family members, the values you choose, and the amount of overlap between top values.

The Wray's Family Values Matrix

	Generosity	Travel	Education (2)	Spiritual Growth	Comfort at Home (2)	Friends	Financial Security
Generosity							
Travel							
Education (2)							
Spiritual Growth							
Comfort at Home (2)							
Friends							
Financial Security							

Now take a small break—brew up some tea, play a card game, or go for a walk.

Break over?

Okay, now we move on to the next step in completing the matrix, which requires filling in all the spaces by answering the following question: How compatible is each item at the top of the chart with the item at the side of the chart?

For the things that complement each other (for instance, generosity enhances spiritual growth—and vice versa), put a plus sign (+) in the chart space; for the values that work against each other (for example, financial security loses ground when you "travel" on vacation), fill in a minus sign (–). Some things may not be clearly complementary or antagonistic, but if you're creative and put some thought into it, you can find positive or negative links. If it's an equal combination of both, simply put 0. This step will, I hope, prompt lots of good discussion about each of the items.

Before totaling everything, look at the items that have numbers by them. (For the Wray family, education and comfort at home both had 2s.) When these complement another value (for example, education and travel are complementary), that space in the matrix gets two pluses.

Now that the family has a big chart with lots of pluses and minuses, it's time to add up the results and decide which of the many values will prevail.

Go down each column and add up the number of plus signs and subtract the number of minus signs. Don't worry if any values get negative numbers. You've already decided that they are important; now you're just observing how compatible they are with other things you treasure.

When the Wrays totaled up their numbers, they found that their top values are education (net score of 6), spiritual growth (net score of 5), and friends (net score of 4). The second chart shows the Wray's completed matrix (see p. 51).

This family choice of top values can now be used to settle many debates and determine family direction. Let's say that Jay would like to join a men's softball team that plays each week during the time of his family's religious service. One glance at the family's value statement and he knows he must find a team that plays at a different time. Spiritual growth comes first. Or if Kristin and Basjana would like to take a summer vacation to Europe, but would need to dip

The Wray's Family Values Matrix—Completed

	Generosity	Travel	Education (2)	Spiritual Growth	Comfort at Home (2)	Friends	Financial Security
Generosity	N/A	–	0	+	–	+	–
Travel	–	N/A	++	+	–	0	–
Education (2)	–	++	N/A	++	0	0	++
Spiritual Growth	+	+	++	N/A	0	+	0
Comfort at Home (2)	–	–	0	0	N/A	++	–
Friends	+	0	0	+	++	N/A	0
Financial Security	–	–	++	0	–	0	N/A
Total + and –	–2	0	+6	+5	–1	+4	–1

into Kristin's college fund to cover the cost, they'll see very quickly why that's not in line with what the family knows it values.

At first glance these results may seem problematic, because no one wants to give up financial security (which in the Wray's case did not make the top three), or any other important value. But the nice thing about this system is that none of the three main values work *against* monetary stability, and, in fact, education actually supports it in the long run!

This same matrix method can be used by any family, of any configuration, with the voting members each contributing top values to the matrix. You'll notice that this exercise works particularly well with the Wray household because there are more parents than children in this house. Even a single parent of very young, nonvoting family members can use this chart to visualize how the chosen values will affect each other. In the case of families where the children greatly outnumber the adults, you run the risk of having the voting be heavily biased toward such goals as "lots of candy"! In these cases, the matrix can be altered by adding extra weight to an adult's values or by having all the children decide their top three among them, using the same matrix for themselves. Remember, as the Executive Parenting Team, you get to make the rules, but also try to remember that rules should be made clear beforehand, not after your children have chosen values you don't want on the list.

SECRETS FROM RESEARCH
Scruples Is Not Just a Game

There's a game on the market called Scruples that can help you sort through some of these questions of values. In the process of playing the game, you are asked a series of "What would you do if . . ." questions that can help you figure out in a playful way what really counts. I remember once getting the question, "Would you pose naked for a magazine for $10,000?" It ended up that I valued modesty over money, but everyone in the group asserted that I would have done it if I had been offered more money!

THE FAMILY MISSION STATEMENT

Now that you've settled on a ranking of family values, you hold a precious key that will guide your decisions, your actions, your family beliefs and principles. This important information should not be kept on a scrap piece of paper. Turn the result of your hard work into a family document—a Family Mission Statement—that is prominently displayed in your home.

You might choose to do this with fancy scroll calligraphy in an elaborate frame, or you might rather hand-print the list and use a magnet to hold it to your refrigerator. The point is, this list should be visible to all family members and be in a place that is easily accessible when decisions have to be made.

The Wray family decided to use their computer to create a formal-looking paper that now is framed and hung in the kitchen over the table, where all are reminded every day of what they value. It's reproduced here to give you an idea of how you might do something similar.

WRAY FAMILY MISSION STATEMENT

We, the members of the Wray Family, hold certain values in high regard. We use these agreed-on values to guide our actions and our family decisions. We look to these values to bond us together as we move forward into a future and build our family on a foundation that will support us in times of joy and in times of trouble.

Among all others we choose these top values:

    Spiritual growth

    Education

    Friends

Signed on this day of 1 June 20xx

Jay Wray: _____

Basjana Wray: _____

Kristin Wray: _____

CHANGING VALUES

As is true of all mission statements, it will be important to review and adjust your prioritized values as your family grows, ages, and changes. The values that guide a couple living together are likely to change when they get married, and then change again when they have children, and then change again when the children go to school, and so on throughout the life of the family. You'll notice that I suggested writing out your mission statement on paper, not carving it in granite. Keep your values and goals flexible enough to move around in the ordered list, but firm enough to be a guiding presence in your family. Remember that from time to time you'll need to go back to the drawing board.

Take Mike for example. After college graduation, Mike moved in with his fiancée, Sasha, and got a job in the highly competitive world of Wall Street finance, planning to be a multimillionaire by age thirty. Working long hours, wining and dining clients late into the night, and spending weekends on the golf course all fit into his plan for financial success. A few years later, after the wedding and a newborn son, Mike felt the need to work even harder to provide for them. He valued his ability to buy them a home and make them feel financially secure. Later, after two more children had come along, Mike accepted a promotion that involved traveling, and he spent even more time away from home. Sure, he wanted to teach his kids how to throw a football, but the peewee coach did that for him. Mike, for his part, was acting on his belief that financial security was a top priority in his family. And maybe Mike's values also included a bit of unspoken pride, ego, competition, and other personal characteristics.

Over time, the hole in Mike's gut (which two different anti-ulcer medications tried to hide) and Sasha's persistent complaints were telling them that their values were changing. The happiness of their growing family was on the line. If family members let life push them in directions that don't match their changing priorities, they simply cannot find happiness. When a captain starts out in his ship heading toward the Grand Caymans, but decides instead to go to Martha's Vineyard, a course change is necessary. Similarly, Mike and Sasha needed to make a course change; they needed to stop and talk about what they valued and how they could best live those values.

After a long phone conversation, Mike and Sasha agreed that time together as a family now had more value to them than their desire to live like millionaires. Before the year was out, Mike took a salaried job at a local bank, left work every day at 4:30 to coach his children's various sports teams, and spent his weekends working around the house, running errands, and helping Sasha transport their three kids to and from all their activities.

Even after these arrangements were made, some fine-tuning was necessary. Household expenses needed to be adjusted, and, even with that, it wasn't easy to make ends meet. They both agreed that Mike might use some of his skills to do some independent financial consulting, but would limit it to less than ten hours a week.

Today, twenty years later, Mike confesses that he still hasn't let go of his wish to be a multimillionaire and is sometimes surprised that he dropped out of that race for wealth. "But," he says, "I made that choice with the support of my wife, and I know that has made us both rich in many other ways. It has definitely given a better life to my children—and they have always been my priority. I don't regret making that career change. Besides, I just postponed that dream. I may be a millionaire yet!"

What about the men and women Mike worked with in the early days who didn't drop out of the rat race? Are they unhappy? Did their families suffer? Well, that depends on their family values. There are some families who decide that personal wealth is very important to them and that the payoff is well worth the sacrifice of family time together. In those cases, it's likely that we'd find a happy family there too. The key is knowing what your family values are and making decisions based on that knowledge.

There are many elements that make a family happy. Shared values—whatever those values may be—create an important and powerful bond that helps a family stick together. When you layer on commitment and communication, as you'll see in Secret 2, you've got the makings of some great family glue!

Happy Families . . . Commit and Communicate

There's probably a time in every boy's life when he dreams of being a professional baseball player. For me, that dream lasted only about one week, and the reason is simple: I stunk at baseball!

Nonetheless, like all my boyhood friends, I headed off to the local school yard every afternoon for practice, and week after week I fielded grounders and fly balls, threw the ball around the bases, and stood at the plate to bat. Even though I never made it beyond Little League, I paid close attention to the instruction my coaches offered. Now, long after I've hung up my mitt and put away my ball, there is one lesson that I still remember: "Follow through."

If you've never had the chance to take lessons in baseball (or tennis or bowling, for that matter), here's the crux of the lesson. When you swing the bat and make contact with the ball, you shouldn't stop the swing at the moment of contact; as the ball leaves the barrel of the bat, you should continue the swing, moving your arm up toward your opposite shoulder in a continuous arc.

Before you check the front cover of this book to see whether you accidentally picked up a book called *Things I Learned While Playing Baseball*, stick with me. This lesson does relate to the secrets of happy families.

Physics tells us that the trajectory of the ball coming off the bat is determined by the full arc of the swing. To us amateur players, it simply means that if we stop our swing at the moment of contact, the ball falls dead because it doesn't have the power of the swing behind it (that's why a bunted ball won't make it out of the infield). Anyway . . . it's the follow-through of the swing that gives direction and power to the ball as it leaves the bat.

That, at last, brings us to relationships. Meeting and falling in love are indisputably important foundations for establishing a new family, but the direction and power of your relationship are determined by what you do after you have made contact—after you've made a commitment to another person to create a family. At that point, the way to give your relationship enough power to get out of the infield is to swing with all you have and follow through with a heartfelt commitment to stay together.

It's really no secret at all that happy families work hard to stay happy, but that means that the parents in that family work hard to stay together! This togetherness factor was recognized by many of the respondents to the Happy Family Survey. When asked what they thought was the most important factor in maintaining a happy family, resiliency took the top spot, but more than 26 percent said that growing up with one's biological mother and father was of principal importance. Clearly many families give high priority to the benefit of having parents and children stay together.

Want to build a happy family? Commit to your partner for the long run and absolutely refuse to quit.

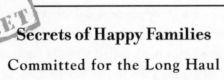

Secrets of Happy Families

Committed for the Long Haul

My four children are happy and secure, I believe, because they know that their parents love each other and are committed to one another for the long haul. In our throwaway marriage culture, my two oldest children (eight and seven years old) have both watched their friends weather the storms of their parents' divorces. Suddenly, they became terrified that every snippy comment my husband and I made to one another meant that a divorce was imminent. I'm so thankful that they voiced their concerns to us rather than hide their fears; we've been able to assure them divorce is simply not an option for us. When we got married, we promised God that we'd be together until death; this is a promise we've reiterated to our children as well. It's also been good for them to see that, even though their friends' parents have divorced, their children are still completely loved by each parent.

—*Jennifer, 33, married 11 years*

WHAT EXACTLY DOES "COMMITTED" MEAN?

When two people decide to form a family, they make a commitment to each other: *I choose you to be my life partner.* In most research on happy families, that commitment is assumed to be in a marriage—and for a good reason. Studies show that people who are married are, on average, happier than single, separated, divorced, or cohabitating families.[1]

However, I know that there are many happy families that include unmarried couples. There are a host of legal, medical, financial, and personal reasons that can force a committed couple to join together outside the bonds of matrimony to form their family. Moreover, there are social reasons why people choose not to marry. When I talk with such couples, I can clearly see that the key to their happiness and longevity is in their honest commitment to making a life together, regardless of their legal marital status.

The Many Faces of Couples

Peter and Jim have been together for thirty years and have enjoyed the comfort and pleasure of their extended family, which includes

Peter's daughter and granddaughter (and of course their dog, Marcus). They have long ago passed through the romantic stage of their relationship, and have weathered the ups and downs of the middle years. I have no doubt that they will spend the rest of their lives together despite the fact that New York will not allow them to marry. They are a committed couple.

Bella and Simon are two doctors without children who decided to move to New Hampshire and buy a house together, but not to marry because the tax liabilities would be too great. They also are very committed to each other and view themselves as married, although not legally so.

Peter and Jim and Bella and Simon are good examples of how commitment, so vital to a couple's happiness, is not exclusive to any one kind of relationship. Certainly, the couples that make up the American family are a varied group. You, for example, if you are in a couple relationship, may be married with biological or adopted children (or both!); you may be married with step- or foster children; you may be unmarried but cohabiting with biological or stepchildren; you may be gay with adopted children, or you may be a lesbian with biological, step-, or adopted children. Whew! And there's probably some variant of these combinations that I've left out. But here's the thing: whatever your couple status may be, if you expect to build a happy family, the best way to do so is to make a long-term commitment to your partner.

Commitment Shy?

I emphasize this point about long-term commitment because I know there are many families composed of unmarried couples who choose to stay unmarried because they are (consciously or unconsciously) afraid to make that long-term commitment. These are the couples who live together and then split in record numbers, leaving behind unhappy and confused children. In my experience as a therapist, I've seen the same pattern over and over again: those who have the legal right and opportunity to marry but who choose instead to "play house" have trouble establishing the ties of a happy family over time.

Occasionally I meet couples who hold back on making a formal commitment, asserting that they don't really need a piece of paper or a commitment ceremony (in the case of gay couples) to tell everyone else what they already know. Other couples resist formalizing a relationship because they believe that getting married will increase the risk of splitting up. Not being "stuck" will force them to be better to each other, they reason. Could be, but not according to the research facts.

According to statistics, the decision to marry or not to marry does have an impact on the longevity of the relationship. The latest findings from the National Center for Health Statistics say that the odds of a marriage ending within five years is 20 percent, whereas the chances of an unmarried cohabitation breaking up is a whopping 49 percent in that same time. After ten years, that separation rate rises to 33 percent for a first marriage, compared to 62 percent for cohabitations.[2]

If you are cohabiting with your partner even though you could marry if you wanted to, then for the sake of your family, I wholeheartedly encourage you to marry.

But whether you do or do not marry, or whether you legally and financially can or cannot marry, if you are a couple, the strength of that commitment will form the foundation of your family—and the foundation of your family's happiness as well.

COMMITTED THROUGH THE YEARS

When we choose to commit our love and fidelity to another person for life, we all need to remember that this promise extends even into the future when the heart-stopping thrill of the early years starts to fade. In case you're reading this book early on in a relationship, I don't want to be the first to break it to you, but the "Oh my god I can't live another minute without that person in my life" feeling doesn't stay with you forever. The loss of this head-over-heels feeling happens to every couple—but that's no reason to panic and bolt.

Love is not a constant entity; it grows, changes, ebbs, and flows throughout the life of a relationship. Those of us who know and accept this are much more likely to hang in there during the tough times and be rewarded with something much more powerful than the rush of new love.

The Beginning

When two individuals who are attracted to each other meet and fall in love, they are barraged with a mix of brain neurochemicals that causes a giddy, almost obsessive attachment to each other. In this period of love, called the romance phase, each of the lovebirds pays attention selectively to the qualities that are turn-ons. Moreover, romance helps them remain blind to the faults of the lover. To sweeten the pot, this flood of brain chemicals actually causes each partner to be more giving, more attentive, and more energized. As a result, when individuals first fall in love, they behave in ways that bring out their best qualities, and they see positive qualities in their partners that may not even exist.

Do you remember those days? You couldn't wait to be in the physical presence of your lover again. You could actually stare at him or her all afternoon and come back tomorrow for more. You found yourself grinning at work as your mind wandered to thoughts of what the two of you would be doing that night. Love was absolutely thrilling, all-consuming, and just plain fun.

The human species has this early romantic stage to thank for its very existence. In the beginning of your relationship, the neural brain circuits hold back information that would ordinarily make you aware that the object of your affection tends to be a bit lazy, or often forgets important dates, or really should take better care of his or her personal appearance. Instead, a flood of "feel-good" dopamine from the brain feeds those feelings of ecstasy, giving you the time needed to bond with a mate in order to ensure the survival of the human race. Quite ingenious really. But also rather deceptive: this early stage of enthrallment passes—at just about the time many couples have already had sex and are about to expand their family.

The Middle

Ideally, "love goggles" and attentive behavior would last throughout the life of the relationship. But they don't. As the memories of those wild, uninhibited, carefree, boundless days of romance fade into the distance, couples begin to settle into routine family life. Unless they have taken a marriage education course, they rarely at that point consult each other about expectations; they seem to have done such a good job of being happy while dating that they figure they'll keep on being happy. Right? Well, not always.

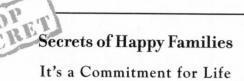

Secrets of Happy Families

It's a Commitment for Life

When we got married, we decided that my job would be to raise our four children and my husband's job would be to secure the family financially. We've made conscious decisions to manage our expenses so I will never have to work again, so long as we have children in the house. Although this is sometimes tough for me professionally speaking (I have a master's degree in education), I know this is the best decision for our children. Realizing that you've made a commitment for life helps you not worry about the little things that could get bigger. In the grand scheme of things, you'll always be together, so one way or the other everything works itself out.

—Keli, 35, *married 4 years*

Subtly, things start to change. A few crying kids, a career disappointment, overdue bills, a broken faucet, or a class reunion that stirs up an old flame—suddenly this family thing starts to be a drag. And adding to the plummeting disappointment, the brain chemicals that supported blind romantic love are subsiding.

Numerous studies show that romantic love does indeed fade with time. But you probably didn't need a study to tell you that. As the luster wears off, couples move into a transitional phase; if they are not prepared for this transition, it can threaten the very future of the relationship. Many conflicts emerge in this phase of the relationship (we'll read more about that in Secret 6).

People who have the mistaken impression that having arguments is evidence that they've picked the wrong partner may begin to consider separation or divorce once this phase hits. In fact, the highest divorce rate is in the first year of marriage; the second highest rate is during the second year; the third highest rate is in the third year.[3] In my experience, the marriages that go on to many decades of happiness together and the ones that end in the first few years are not totally different types of marriages; it's just that the ones who are still married stuck through the rough times, decided to stay in the game, and had reached the point where they learned how to love being married to each other.

Once the romantic phase winds down, couples develop a slow-growing and much deeper bond with each other. This downshift in intensity prepares two individuals for love over the long haul, and it reinforces a lasting sense of companionship. It's the kind in which being together now causes different brain chemicals, vasopressin and oxytocin (hormones involved in bonding) to create feelings of attachment and contentment. This is what happens over the daily morning cup of coffee, through years of understanding each other's needs and quirks, and after you've learned to finish each other's sentences. This kind of love is lasting, and if accepted and cherished, will be the glue of your commitment.

If you can't face the disappointment of losing those intense romantic feelings and refuse to give up the idealized picture of your mate, then you're likely to stumble when it's time to move on to the next phase.

For example, Harold came to me totally flummoxed with disappointment eight years into his fourth marriage. He began all his previous marriages (none of which lasted for more than four years) like this one, feeling incredible passion for his brides. He was outgoing, energized, and bubbling over with emotional and sexual energy.

Yet in each case, he began to feel the magic vibes from the beginning of the relationship fade. In his first three marriages, he concluded that in some way the marriage was flawed, and that there must be another person in the world who would help him get that feeling back. In this current marriage, his longest, he had had the same initial rush of positive feelings. But alas, once again it was fading. Now, by his choice, he barely had sex with his wife and lacked any sense of emotional connection to her. In our first counseling session, he raised the possibility that perhaps he's just the kind of person "who should not be married."

Although Harold's experience of going from euphoria to despair four times is somewhat extreme, I wouldn't say that he shouldn't be married. Rather, I'd say that he simply doesn't understand how love works, so he is constantly disappointed by his unrealistic expectations.

Harold could learn a great deal from a conversation I had with a local woman who clearly understands the changing faces of love. Margaret has been married to Jake for ten years—her second marriage, Jake's first. She told me that her secret to keeping her family strong, secure, and happy was her sense of gratitude for the deep and mature kind of love Jake has given her. It seems that at the young age of twenty-five, Jake asked Margaret to marry him and to bring into his life her two boys from her previous marriage. "I fall in love with Jake all over again," she says, "every time he goes out of his way to be a good parent to my kids."

Margaret told me that she used to worry that he might change his mind when the fun of being a couple in love started to get watered down by the job of running a household with two rambunctious boys.

"But over the years," she says, "he's proved over and over again that his love for all of us goes so far beyond that kind of giddy and passionate feeling of new love. Our family gets closer every day, and I think that Jake's commitment to us is the reason for that. I don't worry anymore that he'll get tired of us—we've all become a part of each other."

That's the glue I was talking about.

If you've reached this middle stage with your partner, here's a secret that can help you avoid the kind of disappointment that plagues people like Harold: rethink your expectations. If your dating days were full of fireworks, like the Fourth of July, expect your middle years to be more like the fifth of July. Never thought much about the fifth of July, did you? But it happens just as often as the Fourth does!

It might seem depressing to think that you're in an "ordinary" phase of your love relationship, but even the fifth of July can be fun—if you make a conscious effort to bring back some of the excitement of the early days. This is the finding of Arthur Aron, a professor of social psychology at the State University of New York at Stony Brook.[4] In his clever experiment, his research team compared two groups of married couples. To one group, he assigned the task of simply walking back and forth across a room. The couples in the other group were also told to go across the room, but they had to do so on all fours, with their wrists and ankles bound together, pushing a ball!

After the experiment, couples were asked questions about the level of connection and love they felt toward their spouse. The couples who had done the more challenging tasks together felt closer to their partner than those in the comparison group felt. The researchers hypothesized that long-time couples can get some spark back in the relationship by occasionally replacing the familiar and predictable with something new and exciting.

You don't have to get out ropes and chains to feel reconnected to your mate (although you can if you want). Some things, as simple as dinner at a new restaurant or a day trip to someplace never visited before by either partner, can release dopamine, sparking a renewed sense of happiness.

Happiness research shows that attitude matters. You dictate your own level of happiness and have an exceptional degree of control over how many times you'll feel joy today—and how many times you attempt to make your partner feel joy.

So what can you do today—not tomorrow—to up the happiness level in your relationship, now in its middle stage? Even though you're both tired, overextended, and not quite as starry-eyed as you were when you were dating, you can still capture some of that old joy.

So do you have any plans in mind? Maybe a return to some activity you used to do in the beginning of your relationship that would be new again if you did it now. Maybe you loved to surprise your partner with flowers or a love note or a gift to celebrate absolutely nothing. Maybe you enjoyed making a favorite dinner that you haven't made in years because the kids don't like it. Maybe you slipped your hand down his or her pants when you were sitting at a banquet table. Or maybe you can begin something brand new that will increase your level of satisfaction. Perhaps a visit to the nearest casino? Amusement park? Ski trail? Art museum? Circus? Or even just stroll in a new park where you can buy a hot dog from the man with the umbrella cart on the corner. These are things you can still do, no matter how hectic your life has become.

Having a clear understanding of the ways love changes, grows, and renews over time will help you maximize the love, security, strength, and happiness it can give to your family life—if you make the effort to keep that spark alive.

And in the End . . .

Mark Twain once said, "Love seems the swiftest, but it is the slowest of all growths. No man or woman really knows what perfect love is until they have been married a quarter of a century."

There's something in Twain's advice for all of us. That's why when I read divorce stats, I cringe to think that many couples will never experience the deep, spiritual, and harmonious love of a long-term relationship because they dropped out too soon.

Remember the Paul Masson motto, "We will sell no wine before its time"? Oenophiles around the world know that the quality of wine changes with age, and the most treasured wines are those that have mellowed over time and have lost the sharp edges of youth. If only we could enjoy and savor in the same way the changes that occur in our personal relationship with our partner over time. Although different from the early days of infatuation, passion, and fireworks, long-term love gives us a bond that has depth, comfort, and deep satisfaction. You can get drunk on that kind of relationship!

Secrets of Happy Families

The Importance of Respect, Love, and Passion

I believe the most important factor for a happy family is the "framework," in other words: the parents. You and your spouse need to be truly committed to each other. Your marriage must be strong and healthy. I cannot possibly believe my family would be as wonderful if my husband and I did not treat our union with the respect and love and passion that we both put into it every day. Our five children can only reap the benefits.

—*Samantha, 40, married 14 years*

If you're lucky enough to know a couple in this climactic stage of their relationship, you can learn a lot by watching the way they interact with each other, almost as if they were one person. But be careful about taking advice from them about building a partnership that holds up over the long haul. An interesting phenomenon occurs once folks reach the mature phase of their love: they forget about the middle phase! That's why younger couples are tricked into thinking that their marriage is faulty when they have an argument—many older relatives and friends will say that such disagreements never came between them and their loved ones. Nonsense!

Almost every couple has conflict that can nearly destroy a relationship. Individuals who split up with their partners remember every detail of those conflicts, but the ones who stay together allow those memories to fade over time because they always have new shared experiences ahead of them and new happy memories that smooth over all rough edges.

These couples not only have had more time to savor the stories of their past but also seem to have had more years to build happier and healthier memories in the future than their peers who remain single or divorced. A recent study that tracked mortality rates found that unmarried people were 58 percent more likely to die during the study period than their married counterparts.[5] A strong reason for this difference seems to be that the lifestyle changes naturally following marriage (less late nights drinking and smoking with friends, for example) lower the rates of cardiovascular disease, cancer, and respiratory diseases. Other studies have shown that married people have lower rates of all types of mental illnesses and suicide.[6] This later-love phase is good for the body and soul—for those patient enough to wait for it.

Although the later years in a long-term partnership are certainly easier than the middle years might have been, I'm not foolish enough to claim that they are entirely conflict free. People don't stay in this comfort zone every minute of the day during the whole of their union. In most relationships there are bumps along the way.

However, as the relationship matures, these troubled times tend to be less forceful and disruptive and to pass more quickly than upsets of earlier days. The concrete foundation for the devotion, loyalty, and commitment of a happy family has been poured; it has settled and been tested. It is now quite resilient.

COMMUNICATION: THE TOP SECRET OF HAPPY COUPLES

Given that staying together as a couple is important to the quality of a happy family, it's certainly worth learning a few techniques and strategies that can help you do that. I've written two whole books on this subject. But in this book, with only one chapter focusing exclusively on the couple relationship, I've had to ask myself, *If I had to choose the one strategy for building a strong relationship that stood out from the others, which one would it be?* The answer didn't have to come from the inner recesses of my mind; it came from my survey.

When I asked couples about the factors that mattered most in families, I provided several options but also left room for people to write in answers. The most common write-in vote was *communication*. Or, in the words of forty-five-year-old Dikendra: "Communication, communication, communication and, of course, communication. Oh, let's not forget the most important: communication." Think she was trying to tell me something? Of course, many of the adults in the survey were describing general communication within the family. I'm on board with that. But if you can't learn good communication styles as a couple, you'll have a hard time imparting them to your offspring.

What Exactly Is Communication?

You may be thinking, *If so many people wrote in "communication," why wasn't it one of the survey choices?* It is simply because communication has too many different definitions, and offering the simple word "communication" on a multiple-choice survey might have resulted in misleading conclusions. Many people think "talking to each other" means communication, and it does. But how come when I tell my wife, "Of course I'd love to go T. J. Maxx with you, honey!" she gets upset with me? Because she knows I really don't want to go to the store, and she can hear it in my tone. So I guess tone is also another way to communicate. Spoken words, verbal tone, and written messages are all ways of communicating.

In fact, the form of communication with the greatest impact is in what we say—without a word.

Communicating Without Words

I first saw examples of powerful "nonverbal couple talk" early in my life while watching my hands-down-favorite TV show, *Mutual of Omaha's Wild Kingdom*. Yeah, now you know I'm ancient, but I like to think that my advanced age gives me perspective. Anyway, back in the 1960s, every week the host introduced me to new animal species whose members very often had fascinating ways of relating to each other. Usually it involved sticking their noses in some body cavity, but depending on the animal, it could include ramming heads, showing off colorful plumage, or picking through the other's hair for little bugs. There was no doubt in my mind that these animals were connecting with each other through their actions in a far more direct and intimate way than they would even if they did possess the power of speech.

Which brings me to human animals. Humans are rare among animals in that their main mode of connecting is through verbal interactions: e-mails, phone calls, letters, songs, and heart-to-heart conversations that continue well into the night. And they are the only species to commit their speech to the written word. So it's natural to think that communication = words. But it ain't necessarily so.

Take it from a guy who makes his living by asking couples to talk about their relationships: just because someone is uncomfortable using words to express feelings and needs, even joy and appreciation, doesn't mean that the person isn't communicating.

Although men and women may not show their feelings by ramming heads or showing off colorful plumage, they sure can communicate profound feelings through their actions rather than their words. How? To borrow a line from Elizabeth Barrett Browning, let me count the ways:

1. Holding hands
2. Giving back rubs and neck rubs
3. Looking at each other from across the room
4. Crying in a partner's arms
5. Letting a partner cry in his or her arms
6. Buying gifts or sending cards
7. Taking the spider out of the living room while the other stands on the sofa with her (or his!) eyes screwed shut
8. Offering a coat or jacket to help warm up a partner
9. Having a cup of hot chocolate ready when a partner comes in from shoveling the walk

These examples of nonverbal language are endearing ones that we all need to use more often and need to be on the lookout for when they're used by our mates. But nonverbal communication is not always the language of love. Scowling at your mate's social faux pas, pacing by the door waiting for your partner to pick out just the right outfit for a simple dinner out, and looking the other way when he or she tries to get your attention are also all forms of communication.

I'm sure you already know that these negative forms of communication are a lot less beneficial to the health of your relationship than the positive ones. In fact, they can be downright destructive—even to your physical health. Researchers found that "negative marital interactions," including nonverbal clues like eye-rolling, lead to decreases in immune function. In fact, James Coan, a neuroscientist from the University of Virginia, concludes, "How often someone rolls their eyes at you can predict how often you need to go to the doctor."[7]

Dr. John Gottman has used his "Love Lab" to quantitatively assess what happens in marriage, and finds that couples continuously send each other "bids" all the time (both verbal and nonverbal)—up to a hundred times over a simple dinner. The bid may be any spoken statement ranging from "You're cute!" to "When did the gardener come?" And it can be a nonverbal statement, such as a sigh, a downtrodden look, or a raised eyebrow. Simply put, a bid is an effort to draw the other person into a connection. It's the first step in communication.

How a person responds to a bid is one way of determining the quality of the relationship. Husbands in stable relationships ignore 19 percent of their wives' bids; husbands headed for divorce ignore them 82 percent of the time. Women tend to be better at responding to bids, ignoring only 14 percent if they're likely to stay married and 50 percent if they are headed for divorce.[8]

So to strengthen your family life today, focus on your patterns of nonverbal communication with your partner. Keep count of how many positive signals you send versus the negative ones. Assuming that you're shooting for the ideal five-to-one ratio of positive gestures (smiling, laughing, giving high-fives or "bumps," and nodding agreement) to negative (ignoring, sneering, eye-rolling, glazed-over expression), the result of one day's tally will give you a good idea of where you stand on the communication issue—regardless of whether or not you sit down to have those heart-to-hearts.

The Gender Difference

This is the twenty-first century—a time when scientific, biological, and genetic studies make it very clear that men and women do not think, act, or feel the same. On some level, most happy couples know this. Looking at your communication style as a man or woman is a good place to start evaluating your communication strengths and weaknesses.

Of course, in this discussion of gender differences in communication, I am talking in broad generalities. Certainly, not every man or every woman will fit into one neat category. I've treated many women who love to get under the hood of their husband's car and change the oil; I've treated men who can spend hours choosing skin-care products for themselves, much to the chagrin of their wives. But still, there are some observations about general gender differences in communication styles that are worth considering.

For example, one couple who'd been working hard on their relationship came into my office to discuss communication breakdown. Cindy was a bright businesswoman who worked internationally teaching others how to set up social services for children. Yet in each session, she lamented that her personal relationship continued to stall out. Why?

Well . . . Cindy was quite certain that it was "because Phil and I never have any meaningful talks. I just can't get him to open up."

When it comes to strengthening communication skills between heterosexual partners like Cindy and Phil, a little biology lesson is often helpful—many of the communication problems I see in my practice are rooted in genetic gender differences. I admit that I've been accused in the past of perpetuating stereotypes by saying that females like to talk and men don't. But hear me out on this. This assertion is not based solely on my personal observations (although I have a store of those!). The female's superior language skills have been scientifically demonstrated through studies of the male and female brain. Knowing about these differences and respecting them can have such a strong impact on a relationship that I place them on the top of my list of things that couples can do to ensure a happy relationship.

To help Cindy understand, I held up the plastic brain that sits on my desk and pointed to all the interconnecting regions of this fascinating organ. What I explained about Phil's resistance to long talks may also help you build a stronger bridge of communication with your partner.

Pointing to my little model brain, I told Cindy that the right side of the brain controls expression and interpretation of emotion. And over on the left side of the brain we have the controls for mathematical, logical, and verbally precise thinking. I then pointed out how the connecting fibers, called the corpus collosum, direct traffic between the two brain hemispheres.

Rather dry, I admit, up this point. But here's where it gets interesting. Studies show that women have a larger corpus collosum than men. Scientists believe that the female's superior "brain bridge" results in more efficient communication of emotional information, allowing the (left) verbal part of the brain to have fast-track access to the (right) emotional brain. (Cindy seemed to like this explanation of superior language development in the female of the species.)

I then approached my white board and drew detailed pictures of the brain pathways, and I described how women have more gray matter—the small brain cells that direct all the nerve information through the cerebrum. I showed her how women's gray matter has more connections between cells, suggesting the ability to multitask in a way that men cannot. I contrasted this to the plentiful white matter in the male brain, which helps guys act quickly, but usually in one direction at a time.

Using this medical information, I detailed for Cindy how, in all probability, Phil's male brain processed her request for a particular type of communication differently than her female brain. His way is not wrong, just different. In other words, talking wasn't necessarily Phil's best mode of communication. In fact, Cindy's pursuing that mode too avidly could interfere with peace and harmony.

Embracing the Difference

So how does knowing all this help Cindy—or you, for that matter? Well, I'm hoping that you and your partner will use this knowledge daily in ways that show an understanding and respect for each other based on your differences. And that is at the heart of the reason why I choose to talk about gender-specific communication skills. Gender differences are a good example of one of the many life instances where we need to accept our partners, warts and all, and to acknowledge that sometimes things that seem like infuriating stubbornness may indeed be simply a matter of hardwired neurological traits. I honestly believe that the happiest couples I know are the ones who accept and embrace the differences between them and work to bridge the gap that these differences can cause.

The advice I then gave Cindy might be helpful to you also: when you talk to your male partner, use shorter sentences and make sure you make your point out front. Once during a presentation I was giving, a member of the audience shared a motto she was given to follow in her work as a scrub nurse. When she was trying to describe a problem to the surgeon, he snapped: "Make it fit on a bumper sticker!" According to this woman, she uses the same approach with her husband.

If you want intimate conversation, you can have it. But you must do a few things to make sure it can happen the way you like

Secrets of Happy Families

It's All About Listening

The most important factor for a happy family is having the ability to really listen, not give advice, just know that a woman's version of the story may take ten to fifteen minutes to get to the point, and not to assume that just because a man has got it in five seconds, that a woman has also.

—*Donel, 35, married 10 years*

it. Because he's inclined to jump in and try to "fix" your problem, start by telling your partner what your expectations are: "I'd just like you to listen to what's on my mind and not try to play devil's advocate—just support me no matter what I say; it's important to me to be listened to and not be corrected."

This kind of preamble to a conversation will make his goal clear and can help direct his attention and reduce his feelings of helplessness. Some women will talk intimately with their husbands when they go for a walk because they avoid the discomfort he may feel when having eye contact over long periods of time. Serving food while you talk helps maintain his attention on the conversation while engaging the action-oriented centers of his brain—it also guarantees that he stays in one place.

I think men also ought to have strategies for good listening skills, as women are more likely to equate verbal communication with caring. I've encouraged Phil to make some changes in the way he communicates with Cindy that I believe can help any male better connect with his female partner:

1. During a conversation, try to stay in one place (that means being present in the room both mentally and physically).

2. Resist the urge to jump into the conversation with recommendations or solutions.

3. Occasionally, make a verbal acknowledgment that you're listening ("Is that so?").

4. Try to maintain eye contact.

5. If you don't know what your partner wants from you during the conversation, ask! Simply inquiring, "How can I be a good listener for you?" will help smooth the way for excellent communication.

Yes, men and women often speak and listen as if they were entirely different species. But by recognizing the differences and embracing the opportunity to learn a "new language," you and your partner will soon better understand each other, and that is a golden key to happiness.

The Gay Factor

Researchers are just beginning to look at how gender roles affect communication between same-sex partners. Although conclusive results are not yet in, studies conducted thus far have offered helpful insights into the family dynamics of gays and lesbians.

Although there is still a lot to be learned about how gay and lesbian couples can maximize their coupling skills, it appears that satisfaction rates in heterosexual and homosexual couples are generally about equal. Some practitioners believe that the social experience of coming out in a society that is biased against them gives gays and lesbians a strong foundation on which they can build a connection to each other. Because they've broken the mold for what "ought to" occur in relationships, they're freed up from societal constraints.

They also seem to have better communication with their same-sex partner than heterosexual couples do. As Esther Rothblum, a professor of women's studies at San Diego State University reminds us, "With heterosexual couples, you really have to translate what your partner is saying because they grew up in different worlds, they were socialized in different ways. That's where same-sex couples have an advantage."[9]

Researchers have found that gender roles are less relevant in these relationships and that most partners tend to gravitate toward what feels natural for them, rather than adhering to conventional patterns. Hence, partners mutually decide on how to share responsibilities, and they may be even more motivated than straight couples to commit to each other as a way of staking a firm place in a culture dominated by heterosexual values.[10]

———————

Evolving as a family requires respect for the differences between individuals, not a push to make everyone the same. Bridging the gap between the different styles of communication allows individuals to form intimate bonds with each other. It can lead to a nod or a wink (or in the case of my wife, a kick under the table) that only life partners will understand. It will lead you to that enviable magic that older couples seem to have when they speak in only half sentences, but know what the other means.

As you work to build your happy family life, work first on your relationship with your mate. With that kind of mutual caring and support in place, you'll both be better able to support each other in times of need by learning to lean.

Secret 3

Happy Families . . .

Lean

The people in the crowd cheer; they rise to their feet clapping and yelling words of encouragement; they shower their praise and good-luck wishes down upon the home team. They scream with joy at success; they maintain hope in the face of possible failure. They give the team members mental and emotional strength and the will to keep going when the odds seem stacked against them.

No, this isn't the Super Bowl. This is a family who is surrounded by folks they can lean on; who want it to succeed; who are there in times of need, in times of triumph, in times of doubt. The supporters are people from the extended family, from a circle of friends, from the community, from the church, mosque, temple, or synagogue.

Happy families know that the ability to lean on others is vital to the health and well-being of each family member. By leaning on others—extended family, friends, community relations, and fellow religious members—we each grow stronger.

NEEDING SUPPORT

Pity the poor baby sea turtle. In the summer months, "pregnant" sea turtles crowd the beaches of Tortola, bury their eggs in the sand, and return to a life of frolicking in the sea. About eight weeks later, tiny turtles hatch, and if they're lucky, they see a few other eggs around them, in varying stages of hatching, before they scurry off to the water's edge. If they're unlucky, they are staring down the gullet of a blue-footed heron, readying himself for a turtle dinner. What the baby turtle won't see, however, is mama turtle (or papa turtle, for that matter). No parents around at all. For as the hatchling makes its way to begin a life in the ocean, it's literally eat or be eaten, sink or swim. And sea turtles aren't the only species that leave young'uns alone in their earliest days.

We humans (and all mammals) are designed to function differently. Every child that is born, helpless and dependent, into the world is meant to be connected to a support system from the first minutes of life and onward. Almost without exception, babies are born with support; in the human community, perhaps more than for any other species we know, that attachment to others constitutes an integral part of a happy life.

SUPPORT FROM WITHIN THE FAMILY

Just walk through the halls of any maternity ward in America, and you'll get an idea of what I mean about the power of family attachment. At any time, there will be half a dozen individuals, sometimes taking shifts, hovering around the bed of a new mama. There, right at that moment, is a snapshot of the future of a happy human child. A mother, and around that mother other adults and children who are part of that child's life.

The immediate family is the core group surrounding a child during those first days of life—a group whose configuration can take many forms: often a father and mother, but in many cases a single mom and her partner or her own mom and sister. In lesbian couples, a mother might be supported and cradled by her girlfriend or wife. In the case of surrogate mothers or mothers who adopt away their babies, the intended parents are nearby, waiting to take on the care and nurturing of the baby. All surround the newborn to convey a message (despite the fact that the child cannot understand the spoken word) that says "We are here for you."

Secrets of Happy Families

Blended Families:
A New Kind of Relative

Defining "immediate family" is no longer as easy as looking for matches in DNA. Blended families often provide great examples of how individuals who make up a home are indeed a family, with all the privileges and responsibilities, no matter what their blood relationship, as illustrated in this story submitted to my Happy Family Survey:

My spouse has always wanted a big family (which he inherited with our marriage). His son loves that when something goes wrong in the house, it's not always him anymore. My son now has a built-in brother (six months younger) that he's best friends with. And my two daughters now have a solid, strong, and supportive father figure (their father died almost three years ago). I have a husband who is a partner in our relationship, who, as a single father with custody of his son, has experience with cooking, laundry, and child rearing.

—*Ella, 49, married 1 year*

From that moment of birth to the moment of death, we search to answer the question, "Who is this family that surrounds me, and how do they affect the quality of my life?"

Over time, as we answer and reanswer that question, we come to understand the unwritten code among family members: *I may not always like you, I may not agree with the things you do or the decisions that you make, but I will always be here for you when it matters.*

Take Melinda, for example. At seventeen, she was at the top of her class, and aiming to be the first one in her family to go to college. She was a serious student who usually stayed in at night, but then she met a young man who made her feel special and showed her the fun of an active social life. A few months into the relationship, she found out she was pregnant. When she turned to her boyfriend for support, his affection began to wane, and soon she found out that he had gotten not one but two other girls pregnant at around the same time.

Melinda felt desperate. The boy, whom she assumed would be there for her, was now completely out of her life. Fortunately, her family was there to pick up the pieces. Her mother (who also was unwed when she had her first child at sixteen) now takes Melinda to doctors' appointments, helps her prepare for the birth of her child, and has offered to care for her baby when Melinda returns to school. Melinda's younger sisters are eagerly preparing to become aunts!

Melinda is learning how important the support of family can be.

Secrets of Happy Families

Growing Closer in Times of Sorrow

We have been in the process of adopting for the last two years, and we had a domestic adoption in December. My husband and I got to be present for the birth of the baby and name him. We had the baby for four days when the birth mother changed her mind and took him back from us. We were devastated. I cried so hard and barely left my room. My husband had to take all the baby stuff back. My daughter who was in college came home to be with us and cry with us. It took us about six months to start to move forward again, but we did it as a family. We still talk about the baby on his birthday and pray for him. We are going to continue with our adoption plans, as this has made us all realize that adding another child to our family just feels right. The experience actually brought us all closer because the kids were able to see their parents emotionally raw and how much being a parent means to us.

—Holly, 41, *married 24 years, with two biological children*

When the Family Fails

Of course, not every family abides by the "I'll be there for you" credo. In fact, often I see my clients very distressed over disagreements with family members. These range from sibling rivalry ("Mom loved you best!") to abandonment in times of need. Sarah, for example, is a fifty-year-old woman with one sister and one brother. When Sarah's mother became very ill and her father quite feeble, Sarah moved into the house to provide care for her parents.

Sarah knew she couldn't turn to her brother for help because his own drug problem had caused him to disconnect from the family years earlier. So she hoped her sister, a successful entrepreneur who ran a business thirty miles from her parents' home, would help out. Her sister's response: *I couldn't possibly leave my business, even for a day. You're the one not working right now, so it shouldn't be much of a problem for you to care for Mom and Dad by yourself.*

So that's what Sarah did. Then, three years after her mother died, she took on the care of her ailing father. When his failing health made it necessary to move him to a nursing home, she visited him every day. Her sister came to see him about once a week and, according to Sarah, never once thanked her for what she had done. She did not offer the support that Sarah so desperately needed.

The quality of life for Melinda and Sarah are vastly different because of the quality of their family support. Obviously, when the whole family pitches in together, they become a united team; they feel more cohesive and complete in their participation in the vital functions of the family as a whole. This is one of the big secrets of happy families: the tendrils of support and love extend to all members of the family. And like most good things that are worth having, this kind of support doesn't always come easy. Sometimes being supportive requires a sacrifice of time and personal convenience—reducing feelings of momentary joy, but bolstering that store of deep, long-term happiness for everyone.

A secret of happy families is that they abide by the code of support and caring even if it's at the cost of personal convenience or comfort.

SUPPORT FROM THE EXTENDED FAMILY

When you teach the value of family support to your kids, you must, to the extent possible, model supportive behavior with your extended family as well—which is not always an easy task. Some of my readers may come from families that are not very supportive. Perhaps your parents have disappointed you or have fallen short of ideal. Perhaps you have siblings like Sarah's who don't hold up their share of the family responsibilities or from whom you've grown estranged. Still . . . they are your family, and your partner and your children are watching how you interact with them.

If your father falls ill and needs your help or if your mother has an unexpected hardship and needs financial assistance, what would you do? You can help pave the path to family happiness by teaching the lesson that family ties are lifelong and indissoluble—though occasionally inconvenient. Even when it's not easy, you will show your blood relatives, your mate, and your children how it's done by helping out your own parents without complaint.

Similarly, if you have a sibling who never so much as called when you were in the hospital with your gallbladder attack, what will you do when that sibling himself or herself lands on the sickbed? That's right; you'll send a get-well card and make that phone call. The message you give your loved ones is not "what goes around comes around," but rather "family takes care of its own—no matter what."

Staying involved with all your extended family is a key element in the pursuit of family happiness. In fact, when I'm asked by journalists why people's relationships today are so fragile and why families seem so much more vulnerable now than they used to, most frequently I point to the transient state of the American family.

Secrets of Happy Families

The Safety and Comfort of Home

I think people need a sense of "home and family," a safe base, today more than ever. Our daughter grew up in the same house most of her life, and this is still home—safety and comfort for her—even though she lives in another state. Her husband grew up with multiple divorces and multiple houses. When he thinks about home he doesn't have that comfort or safe base because no one in his family is in the same family, same house, or even the same town anymore. He doesn't have a sense of "home" as our daughter does. He gets a sense of it from our family but wishes it was in his side of the family too.

—*Terrie, 53, married 36 years*

When I grew up, I lived less than a mile from one set of grandparents and fifteen minutes away from the other. My cousins all lived within a ten-mile radius (and those cousins who lived fifteen minutes away seemed to live *really* far away!). If my mother needed to run an errand, my grandmother was there to watch me and my siblings. If my uncle needed someone to look after his kids when he took my aunt to dinner, my cousins were dropped off at our house. This family dynamic was not unique to me; most people over age forty have had a similar upbringing.

One of the secrets of many happy families is that they know they have extended family they can lean on to fill in the gaps—not only in the child-care schedule, but also in the heart and soul.

In Secret 1, with its focus on family values, I told you that the respondents to the Happy Family Survey felt strongly that "resiliency"

Secrets of Happy Families

We Can Get Through This

The greatest gift for a family is giving love and trust to each other—help when needed and always stand by your family. Teach good values and hope we all can live by them. Never turn your back on your family no matter what others may say. Always believe that with your strength and God's help we can get through things together.

—Jo-Ann, 58, *married 39 years*

and "family time" were paramount. But even I was surprised that 55 percent of respondents who had children in the home chose "Living within an hour's distance from children's grandparents" as one of their top five factors for "making a happy family."

In today's mobile world, we can't all be 'round the corner from our parents, aunts, uncles, cousins, and siblings. But we can all make the effort required to keep them nearby in our lives. The telephone, webcams, the Internet, and digital photos all give us the ability to keep in touch, to share our lives, and to give and take support when it's needed.

So whether you're offering to do the grocery shopping for your sister-in-law who just had a new baby, or you're organizing an online support group for her to talk about her joys and worries with family members who love her from afar, you're securing your core of family happiness by reaching out to those you call "family."

This effort to stay connected with family is easy for some people who have strong family ties no matter how great the distance between them. But I also know that reaching out to extended family members can be difficult for others who don't really have that strong family bond. So you might ask, What about those relatives I was never very close to? Or the ones I've lost touch with? Or the ones I never really liked very much anyway? Should I try to reestablish a family connection? Yes, you should. It's definitely in your own best interests.

Renewing Family Relationships

I encourage the effort to keep family ties strong, because there's no good reason not to. It doesn't cost much at all to send a "hello" card to an elderly aunt. It doesn't require a huge investment of time to pick up the phone on your brother's birthday. It doesn't even demand an emotional commitment to extend your hand to an estranged relative who may or may not choose to reciprocate. For those efforts, we gain the possibility of getting so much back. Strengthening a connection with a relative who shares a blood history adds a comforting layer to life that nothing else can duplicate.

That's exactly what happened to my friend Tammy, who recently renewed a friendship with her long-lost cousin, Cliff. Well, not exactly a lost cousin, because she always knew exactly where he lived, but with busy lives and hectic schedules, they just hadn't been in touch for several years.

"We bumped into each other by chance at a local restaurant," she said, "and after our initial hugs and 'how are yous,' we parted with the noncommittal 'Let's get together soon.'"

I've said that myself, and I know how the well-meaning intent rarely turns into a real get-together. But Tammy says she was moved to follow through because of the sense of loss she felt after leaving the restaurant that night.

"Cliff and I had been close as kids growing up," Tammy continued. "And I had heard that he was now making a living as an artist, but I had never seen any of his paintings. So I picked up the phone and asked him to take me to see his work. I think he was surprised, but he agreed to give me the grand tour of the galleries in New York

City. The trip was great fun, but the absolute best part was just being with this person who shares my family history."

With obvious joy, Tammy went on to tell me about their lunch at a small Italian restaurant in Greenwich Village, where she and Cliff sat for a few hours and talked and talked. "I can't describe how good it feels to be with someone who knows things about me and my brothers and my parents that no one else knows," she said. "It's weird, but there's something awfully good about connecting with family. There's no way I'm going to let another ten years come between us."

SUPPORT FROM FRIENDS AND NEIGHBORS

A supportive family certainly makes a family happy. But in most cases, family members can't be the only source of support. It's just too demanding. Too time consuming. To fill in the happiness gaps, we all need friends and neighbors.

The value of a broad support system is clearly seen in a story that was submitted to my Web site by Pam. She explains,

> My mother had a heart attack that kept her in intensive care the two weeks before my youngest daughter was born. I was rushing around trying to keep a vigil by her bedside, care for my two-year-old, run my household, and check in with my own doctor, who was concerned about my rising blood pressure. My husband pitched in the best he could, but he had his own work responsibilities that kept him away from home. Frankly, I don't think we could have made it through that difficult time without the help and love of our friends. Without being asked, they appeared with home-cooked meals, they cleaned my house, they babysat my daughter, they ran my errands,

and they gave us their hugs and prayers. These relationships got us through that time.

I have no doubt that Pam's friends and neighbors made all the difference for her and her husband and daughter in their time of need. But I also will guess that the reason Pam's family received this kind of support is that she had made the effort to build and nurture these relationships in the good times. Surely their ties of friendship were knotted long before they needed an impromptu babysitter.

The Benefits of Reaching Out

Even as I write this I marvel that it has become necessary to encourage families to reach out for friendship. In the old days, when a new family moved into the neighborhood, the Welcome Wagon lady would ring the bell to offer friendship, information, and welcoming gifts. A close friend clearly remembers her first night in a new home as a five-year-old because the memory of the neighbors dropping by with apple pie, casserole dishes, and kind words is still so vivid. I'm hoping there are still pockets of the United States where this kind of welcome is routine, and let's all hope that the tradition will find a rebirth in our country.

One of the unwelcome consequences of the two-income family lifestyle in the digital age is a tendency to choose isolation over socialization. Even the Welcome Wagon business has given up the in-person visits and has moved entirely online! There's little opportunity to get to know our neighbors or to make new friends when so many of us work outside the home and when the automatic garage door opener allows us to enter our private domain without seeing a soul. Even our leisure time creates a disconnect when the TV, video games, and the Internet keep us indoors. Heck, with a Wii I can go golfing, fishing, or bowling without ever stepping outside!

There are lots of economic, sociological, technological, and psychological reasons for pulling in the shutters, but people like Pam

SECRETS FROM RESEARCH
Friends Are Good for You

Want to live longer? Make friends! In his book *The Longevity Strategy*, David Mahoney tells us, "We are inherently social animals. And sociability exerts a positive effect on hormone secretion and the patterning of the . . . nervous system. People who have few social contacts and who report little pleasure in the company of others die prematurely. For instance, survival after heart attack and cancer is lessened in people with few friends."[1]

Compiling further research on this subject, author Robert Putnam reports in his aptly titled book *Bowling Alone: The Collapse and Revival of American Community* that "people who are socially disconnected are between two and five times more likely to die from all causes, compared with matched individuals who have close ties with family, friends and the community."[2]

know that making an effort to build a support network outside the immediate family is vital if we expect to broaden our chances for happiness.

In addition to being a safety net in times of trouble, good neighbors and friends have other benefits as well. Casting out for an eclectic group of friends and acquaintances can give you a better perspective on life in general.

Getting outside the walls of your home with other people who are working to build their own happy families gives you the chance to see that your struggles and challenges are not unique. Often what seems unbearable (such as the way you and your kids argue constantly over what constitutes a reasonable amount of time to play video games in a single day) suddenly seems kind of typical and not worth losing sleep over.

In fact, talking with other parents about their kids or with other spouses about their marriages or with other career people about their work is a great form of therapy. It's very comforting and even energizing to experience that "aha" moment when you realize, "Gee, I'm not crazy after all; other people feel like this too!" or "I'm so glad to hear that someone else does the same thing," or even "Wow, compared to them, I've got it good!"

From others you can learn how different families function, and with that information you can make decisions about what you want to emulate in your own family and what you want to avoid. And this "people watching" does not necessarily have to focus on people who are like you in age, rank, or serial number. Friendships with older couples, for example, can give you insight into how you want (or don't want) your family to develop in the future. You might even find that watching families that have stood the test of time will inspire you and give you hope to persevere through difficulties.

For all these reasons, I feel strongly that if you have a limited social network, you should make the effort to create more ties to more people. Starting today, do something to get to know your neighbors and make more friends: bake or buy a nice cake and stop by your neighbor's door for a good ol' fashioned hello. Or call and ask to borrow something—sugar, eggs, a light bulb, whatever. (Yes, asking for something from neighbors can actually bring you closer to them. People want to feel needed, and they bond to a neighbor who can show a modicum of vulnerability.) Or invite some neighbors over for dessert. It's really quite easy to reach out, and that effort may allow you to receive far more than you give.

SUPPORT FROM COMMUNITY GROUPS

Studies of longevity have repeatedly shown that our connection with others proves to be a life extender. Such compelling data should, no doubt, propel everyone to run out and join a community organization. But that's not what's happening.

From the start of the twentieth century to the 1960s, there was an ever-increasing involvement in civic, church, and community activities (except for the years of World War II). However, over the last two generations, rates of church attendance and at-home entertaining have fallen, and the number of people who get together regularly, from club membership to card games, has fallen by half.[3]

Avoiding Isolation

In an era when running home to catch the latest elimination round on *American Idol* can rob people of a chance to be together as a community, you know that social isolation has got to affect the strength of families. It's through the teamwork and camaraderie of organized groups that we are given an opportunity to gain a larger perspective on life issues outside the walls of our own homes.

SECRETS FROM RESEARCH
Reaching Out for Support

Often it's not possible to look to your neighbors for support, either because of the complexity of the problem or because you haven't established a close enough network of friends. Remember that part of your network can include professional or pastoral counselors who have skills in guiding and supporting you during difficult times. There may also be organizations in your area made up of individuals supporting each other through difficult times (addictions, depression, grief, anger, and the like). These groups provide much-needed support for family members who recognize that their physical or emotional problems can, if left uncared for, severely undermine their efforts to build a happy family.

Moreover, we contribute to a better world through such programs as Habitat for Humanity, Adopt a Highway, or Fight World Hunger. And it is through efforts like these that we pass on to our children an understanding of the value of helping others.

Community groups also help us by offering a host of solutions to local issues. The PTA gives us insight into the educational needs of our children, the gardening club gives us tips for taming those pesky weeds, and the hiking group gives us firsthand exposure to the state of dwindling recreational land and nature preserves.

When families find ways to tie together family mission with community action, it is a sight to behold! During a women's conference in Rhode Island, I had a book table right next to a booth that attracted what appeared to be an endless parade of men, women, teens, and young children. Through the usual polite conversation, I picked up bits and pieces of their story. By the end of the day, I was absolutely in awe of this wonderful group.

The booth was sponsored by the Gloria Gemma Breast Cancer Resource Foundation. I spoke to Gloria's daughter, who explained that the purpose of the booth was to raise money for research and to honor the memory of her mother, who had died of breast cancer. It was staffed entirely by family members of Gloria Gemma, including her nine children and twenty-five grandchildren.

I went home that night and looked online for more information about this interesting family. At their Web site (www.GloriaGemma. org), I found that in describing their mother, this family perfectly illustrated two of the messages I hope to convey in this chapter: "She taught us that, even through tough times, strong families always prevail. . . . She taught us values and the importance of giving back to our community." So this family took those lessons and honored the mother who had taught them by working hard to raise awareness in the hope that other women and men might detect breast tumors earlier than their mother had, and also to raise money needed for vital breast health programs.

Watching the Gemmas work together to help others made me appreciate the profound impact that integration of family and community can make. Of course, we can't all affect our communities on such a large scale, but we can still reach out in some manner.

I saw the lessons of community caring in action at a local town parade. The parade lineup was filled with lots of parents, kids, balloons, and smiles. As the Girl Scout contingent marched by, I noticed that one of the volunteer parent leaders was a woman from town whom I had often seen involved in activities with her four girls—no surprise that she would be a scout leader. Later in the parade, I saw her eldest daughter, Liz, now a teenager, marching alongside her dad as volunteer coaches with a large brood of little softball players running around them.

This is the positive effect of community involvement. We teach our loved ones through example that it's fun to give of ourselves. Instead of sitting at home, isolated in their own rooms, these family members were out enjoying a beautiful afternoon among a community that applauded and cheered their volunteer efforts.

How Can I Get Some of This Community Support?

The more you give of yourself, the more you receive when you need it. So if you want your community to be there for you, get out and get acquainted. If you are not already reaping the rewards of volunteering, here are some quick ideas to get you started:

- If you work outside the home or have children in school, there are lots of opportunities to get involved in charitable activities. (And in the rare circumstance where there are no such activities going on—start some!)

- Look for organized clothing or food drives, fund-raising drives that need supervisors, or any activities that need the time, talent, or treasure your family has to offer.

- If anyone in your family has computer skills, those skills have great value to volunteer organizations. You might offer to create a Web site, write copy, manage content, or maintain or upgrade equipment. Or simply type correspondence or file data.

- Share your time and your talents. Schools, child-care centers, senior centers, teen clubs, and the like often need volunteers to entertain, educate, and mentor.

- Start a community cleanup crew and beautification committee for local parks and school grounds.

- Many senior programs need volunteers to drive members to the store, church, and doctor appointments.

- Many school and town libraries are short on funds and rely on volunteers. You may find you enjoy working among the stacks of books as you assist students or patrons, reshelve returning books, organize fundraisers, or create showcase displays.

 SECRETS FROM RESEARCH
An African American Family Legacy

Historically, extended family living arrangements on all socio-economic levels have been found to be twice as common in African American families than in white families. These extended family members provided economic as well as emotional supports. Despite a history of racial oppression and material deprivation, they have been pivotal in the remarkable resilience and adaptive capacity of the African American family to survive relatively intact despite severe urban conditions.[4]

Volunteering as a family teaches important lessons about what a family is and what you value. So make an effort to join a community with expectations and standards similar to your own. If (after defining your values in Secret 1) you have determined that you value generosity, find friends and groups who are involved in charitable organizations. If you value education, join a book club, get involved in the PTA or PTO of your school, and make connections with other families who do the same. Bring other family members along, and soon you'll see your own happiness increase as you focus your efforts on the happiness of others.

SUPPORT FROM ORGANIZED RELIGION

Of those who responded to my online Happy Family Survey, 37 percent ranked attending religious services regularly as one of the three most important secrets to happy families; 12 percent put it at the top of the list. This surely isn't a majority, but time and again, throughout the survey, it was clear that many individuals included God in their family.

Angel, a thirty-eight-year-old Hispanic man, wrote to me to describe the ordeal of seeing his marriage fall apart: "My wife informed me a week after buying our first home that she wasn't in love with me anymore. We separated for a few months, got back together and then her bad feelings returned, so we separated again."

After a while, Angel and his wife agreed to try to repair the relationship. As he explains, "At the same time, we both rediscovered our faith in God, and we gave it another try and our marriage has been so much better for the past six months. Our passion for one another has returned, we talk much better, and we are recommitted to making our marriage last. We are also in line to adopt our second child. Things couldn't be better."

Jennifer, thirty-seven, also credits her faith for saving her marriage: "In 2004 we suffered an infidelity in the marriage and we divorced. We reconciled in 2005 and remarried one another in

SECRETS FROM RESEARCH
Worshiping in Private

Because religious institutions establish norms for behavior, and because many established religions frown on homosexual sex, one would predict that gay couples would be less likely to integrate formal religious institutions into their lives compared to other couples. That prediction is supported in the findings of my survey, wherein only one-third of the self-identified homosexual respondents ranked "attending religious services regularly" among the top five (of six) values, compared to 69 percent of individuals who were not in same-sex relationships. Judging from the gay clients whom I know, this finding is *not* because gays and lesbians don't wish to integrate religion into their lives, but because they perceive many religious institutions as not wanting to integrate gays into their flock. For this reason, many gay families avoid organized religions, preferring to worship in a personal and private way. However, legal rulings and public sentiment are beginning to act more favorably toward the concept of gay partnership and marriage, and in many parts of the country, social and cultural attitudes are changing.

2006. It was the help and prayers of our church family that put us back together."

How does religion have this kind of power over the quality of a family? Although scientists have spent much time trying to understand the powerful impact of religious beliefs on families, they still can't explain why or how having faith results in an improved quality of life. Maybe that's why it's called "faith." Who can truly understand the mysteries of a Higher Power?

It is clear to me, though, that beyond the direct effects of prayer, participation in religious traditions can help form another layer of "family." Religious beliefs guide the behavior of the members within, and set goals and expectations for those who belong. That's what all families strive to do, and those with the tenets of an organized religion behind them have additional support to move the family in the right direction. Also, organized religion offers a community built on many of the same values held by the member families. This gives all family members a group of understanding people to turn to both in times of trouble and in times of great joy.

Organized religion also offers rituals that solidify our beliefs across generations and throughout our lifetimes—whenever we feel the need for that kind of support. Even those who are not regular churchgoers often utilize this function of religion for the most important family events. Many young adults I went to college with felt they didn't need the church or synagogue in their lives, but when it came to their weddings, there they were, standing at the altar.

In the same way, after marriage, couples often take a hiatus from regular attendance at places of worship, but come the birth of their children, they often again return to religious institutions to help lay the foundation for spiritual beliefs in their children. Even families who steer clear of steeples and minarets often return to the doors of a house of worship when a family member dies.

For many, it is the traditions steeped in religious beliefs that guide them safely through the passages of family life.

All life passages affect the family's need for support from family, friends, community, and religion; a new home, a new job, aging parents, and everyday events add layers of complexity to the family unit. No life passage, however, has the intense impact—both good and bad—of the arrival of children. In Secret 4, you'll see how happy families stay stable through the ups and downs of child rearing.

Happy Families...
Teach to and Learn
from Children

W hen families consider having children, they usually do so
with the heartfelt belief that adding new kids to the clan will
make the family feel more whole, and with the hope that all its
members are moving toward the same goals.

Without a doubt, bringing children into the home results in a
profound enhancement in the richness and complexity of family
life. No one, not one person in the 1,266 respondents who filled out
the Happy Family Survey, said that he or she regretted having children. But everyone who has children knows that the experience of
raising young ones is not always easy. In fact, at times it's downright
agonizing!

Believe me, I know. To this day, I can recall when parental conflict first hit home with Susan and me. Our first child, Matthew, was
just six weeks old when we decided to go to a diner in New Haven,
not far from the hospital where I was working. Keep in mind, I was
a psychiatry resident, so I was chronically exhausted. Keep in mind,
Susan was a new mother who lived hundreds of miles away from
her family, and she was exhausted. So there we were, new mom,
new dad, and new baby, ready to order our first meal together outside the home.

Then, just a few moments after we sat down at our table, our
perfect baby boy started to scream as if he were being attacked by a
band of wild hyenas. Our little Matt didn't have the words to say

Secrets of Happy Families

It's All About Growing Up

I think our children have been the toughest part of our marriage. Parenting brings out a side of yourself and your spouse you don't always like to see. I was a very possessive mom. I didn't like anyone, even my husband, trying to get in the way. That did put a strain on our marriage at times; it still does at times, but we have always figured out a way get through it.

We learned to get along as we matured. I was parent at age sixteen, and for a long time raising children was all I knew. I thought life was all about them, and I did lose myself and started to resent the kids and my husband.

As I get older, I know that I'm worthy of loving not only my kids and my husband but myself. Thank goodness we grow up.

—*Brenda, 36, married 12 years*

what he needed, obviously, but we desperately wanted to give him comfort. So we resorted to checking off the list of things that typically make a baby cry. You know the drill: dirty diaper, gassy pain, uncomfortable positioning, fatigue, hunger, teething. Here's where things broke down. In the game of "guess what the baby needs," I guessed "hungry," and my wife guessed anything but.

You might say, "Well, agree to disagree," but that mantra just doesn't apply here because of one huge problem: the only way to satisfy hunger in our new child was with the magic elixir of mother's milk, and the only place that this could be found was beneath the pads in the specialized bra that Susan was wearing. As the invisible hyenas continued to provoke Matt, we each became more and more agitated searching for a solution. I insisted that Susan nurse him, stating, "If I could do it, I would. But since I can't, I don't see why you won't."

Finally, she did agree, left the dining area, and sat with him on the floor of a tiny bathroom stall. However, Susan was so tense, angry, and exhausted that no breast milk came out. By the time she burst out of the ladies' room in tears, with Matt still screaming, neither she nor I had any appetite. (Presumably Matt still did, but really, who knows?!) The evening ended in disaster, with Susan and me barely talking to each other as we stood just outside the door of the restaurant and ordered some hasty meals to go. Not exactly the joy of parenthood that we had imagined.

Should we be surprised that happiness levels in marriages decline after the birth of a child?

ACCEPT THE CHALLENGE AND REAP THE REWARDS

Opening this chapter with a discussion about how stressful raising children is feels as if I'm writing about the carcinogenic properties of apple pie! Aren't kids supposed to be the very best thing that's ever happened to us? Well, yes, and in fact, most parents do say that their kids are their pride and joy. But it's also true that children often add tension, stress, and upset to the family dynamic. Parents in happy families are able to stay happy even after the kids show up because they know about this phenomenon, expect the disruption, and learn how to deal with it.

The Challenge

So why do the little bundles of joy turn into little generators of tension headaches? Well, the reasons are innumerable. But let's take a look at a few of the most common ways that children can disrupt the serenity of family life.

Children get all the attention. In the heady days of dating, you had eyes only for him or her. And, just as important, he (or she) had eyes only for you! Now that there's a new being in the household, everyone's eyes turn toward the child. Oh—who's that holding the baby? Yeah, that's right, you're the other important person in my life. Sorry, I forgot about you for a minute!

Children take up time. Leisure activities were probably a big part of your life before you started a household. Now, whether it's snowmobiling or reading novels that turns you on, when you are caring for children your time is not your own. Children, at any age, often demand constant time and attention. Whether it's pacing the floors until two in the morning until your baby gets to sleep or driving a grade-schooler from one lesson to another, it's a sure bet that the things you used to do for fun are now long-ago memories, or at least greatly curtailed.

Children are expensive. The average cost of raising an American child from birth to age seventeen ranges from $163,790 (for low-income homes) to $289,390 (for homes with yearly incomes over $75,000).[1] That's for each child! The sacrifices these expenses entail can be downright annoying. (What? I have to give up my daily caramel mocha latte just so little Jimmy can go to college?)

Children are loud and messy. Once kids arrive, you can kiss good-bye your nice clean and orderly life—at least until your child is old enough to follow rules (such as no pouring chocolate syrup on the kitchen floor!). And then he or she may, or may not, choose to obey them.

Children challenge your beliefs. It took you all these years to figure yourself out. Then your children come along and question your values, tastes, and style. They can embarrass you when they express their own beliefs and individuality. They can make you rethink so much of what you thought was absolute in life. And sometimes they make you change your mind about really important things.

Children are individuals. Before our children are born, we have a pretty good idea of what they will be like. They'll be brilliant, loving, attentive, talented—just like we always wanted to be—and will no doubt grow up to be president of the United States. But then your child arrives and instead of loving the violin, she's enamored with drums; instead of swinging a tennis racquet with you, he prefers skateboarding with his friends; instead of enjoying fishing and the great outdoors, she likes video games and punk rock raves. Children have beliefs, values, temperaments, desires, and needs that do not always fall in line with our own hopes and desires.

Secrets of Happy Families

Finding Happiness in Small Things

We were at the peak of happiness when we started trying to get pregnant. We were pregnant within two months. As my belly grew, so did our bond as a couple. We felt as if we were on top of the world. We imagined that our daughter would only add joy to our marriage and make us even happier. If I had known then how much harder and less rewarding having a baby would make our marriage, I think I would have waited a couple more years. But now we have a six-week-old baby and can't turn back.

I try to find happiness in the small things, like my daughter's smiles or when she sleeps long enough for us to have adult time. We've accepted that things will never be the way they were. But that doesn't mean all is lost. We're optimistic that things can be just as good, though different. We say sorry after each fight, say "I love you" often, share in the joy of each baby milestone, and remind each other to slow down, smile, and be good to each other. It's still too early to say what I've learned from raising a child, but I'm already more confident in myself and rather impressed with the support my husband gave me during labor. When we fight now and sleep deprivation makes us both crazy, I remember what an amazing labor coach he was, how he spent two days massaging my back, holding my hand, and feeding me Jell-O . . . and I forgive him for his flaws and shortcomings . . . no one is perfect, though he comes pretty damn close during labor and delivery!

—Cathlyn, 26, married 3 years

So it's no wonder that the apple of your eye can become the source of family stress. One of the secrets of happy families is knowing and expecting that kids—all kids—can disrupt the peace of a quiet household. Take Christine, for example. She's a forty-four-year-old woman, married for twenty years, who resides with her family of seven, including her husband, biological children, and foster children. She had begun working full-time about two years before she completed the Happy Family Survey, and she weighs her current lifestyle against that of earlier years: "While being a full-time wife and mother was the most difficult and thankless job that I ever held, it was definitively the most rewarding, hands down!"

The difference between families like Christine's and the less-than-happy families is that families like Christine's are not shaken up by the chaos that comes with parenthood. When these parents are tossed about in the tornado that is their life, they never forget that the rewards of parenting balance out the challenges.

The Rewards

Just knowing that it's normal for the stresses of raising children to temporarily reduce levels of happiness helps many parents through the tough spots. "Oh thank goodness," they tell me, breathing a sigh of relief. "I'm not the only one who feels that way!"

So if kids can be so problematic, why do we have children at all? (Besides, of course, that part about sex being such a positive experience.) We do it because, despite the trials of parenthood, raising children can be enormously gratifying. The following list names some of the joys and rewards of childhood that are too easily forgotten in the day-to-day work of bringing up baby. You might want to make a copy of this list and keep it handy. The next time you wonder, *What was I thinking?* you'll have the answer.

Children are our hope for the future. They carry on our genes, our values, and our traditions after we are gone. If we've had negative childhood experiences, our own children give us an opportunity to sow new values and behaviors in the hearts and minds of our offspring.

Children bring joy. The wonder and delight of a child are infectious. That heart-warming giggle, that adorable smile, the funny noises and delightful antics—all bring laughter into the home. We bask in their accomplishments, we share their triumphs, we enjoy their adventures. They make us forget our grown-up side and give us so many opportunities to act like children once again.

Children give our life purpose. Going to work every day and cooking a great meal, among other activities, feel meaningful if you know that they are providing sustenance for another being. Children also need us. They give us reason to get up and struggle through another day. They teach us to be more selfless and take a broader view of our role in life.

Children connect us with the community. Having a child brings us into our community. From mother-baby groups or PTO meetings to hanging at the playground with other parents or taking photos at your child's senior prom, when you have children you are no longer isolated; you are a part of the parenting club.

Children connect us to extended family. A child has a wonderful way of bringing together grandparents, siblings, and other family members. When kids are involved, holidays feel more special, picnics more exciting, birthdays more important, and even a family get-together at a local restaurant more interesting. Children can be the family glue.

Children help share the load. In traditional cultures, and still in many families today, children lighten the workload—from helping feed the cows on the farm to filing papers in the family business. But even in those families without a business to support, children shoulder many household responsibilities by completing such chores as vacuuming, raking, shopping, or bringing in firewood for a winter's warmth.

Children give us love. In the first few months of life, your face may be the only one your child knows, and the joy he or she expresses at the sight of it is like no other experience. In childhood, the love your child has for you is pure and honest and comes from the heart. In the teen years, it comes in fits and starts and may even hide for a while. Then in adulthood, it is often given freely with gratitude, acceptance, and understanding. At all ages, children have the potential to give us a lifetime of love in all its wonderful and perplexing forms.

The bottom line is that for many individuals in almost every culture, children and family are like Aunt Jemima pancakes and syrup: they go together. Happy families generally find that the rewards of raising children far outweigh the inevitable challenges. They also realize that parenting doesn't always come naturally and that the skills needed to maintain that delicate balance between joy and anger, pride and disappointment come with time. Here are a sampling of parenting skills often practiced in happy families through each stage of child development.

PARENTING IN STAGES

We tend to talk about good parenting as if we of course all know what that is. But I don't think we do. After all, what's good parenting to one parent is awful parenting to another.

Is it good parenting to send an infant with the sniffles and a slight fever to day care? Probably not, but what if Mom can't miss another day of work without risking being fired? In that case, preserving the economic security of the child may trump the risk of worsening a cold or spreading germs.

Is it good parenting to send a second-grader to school with a toy gun? Certainly not. But does Grandpa know that giving little Mikey a cap gun to show his friends on the playground could put the child and the family in trouble with school rules?

Is it good parenting to allow teenagers to drink alcohol with their friends as long as they all stay in the house overnight and hand over the car keys? Many parents say it is, explaining, "At least we know where they are." Many other parents would argue that allowing underage drinking in any circumstance teaches teens that it's okay to break the law.

Day after day, in any household in America, it's a tough call to say with absolute certainty who is being a good parent and who is not. With that understanding, I'd like to offer some basic parenting tips that have helped many families through the years manage the challenge of trying to be good parents and at the same time creating a warm and happy home.

In the First Months of Life

In early stages of development, children need attention and unlimited love. To get both of these things, they are born with an incredibly effective alarm system—they cry. And cry. That's their only means of communicating important things, such as pain, illness, boredom, hunger, irritability, and fatigue. Yet new parents are often told by well-meaning family and friends, "Don't pick up the baby every time she hollers, or you'll end up with a spoiled baby who cries to be picked up all day long." Well, there goes any chance of having a "happy" family. Who can be happy in a home engulfed in nerve-shattering screams? The human body is programmed to respond quickly to the cries of an infant in distress—ignoring that evolutionary call is very difficult and bound to produce unmanageable stress over time.

Fortunately, this is one word of advice that you can ignore. Instead, you should feel free to keep the peace in your house by comforting your wailing infant. In the first six months, you will not spoil your baby by swiftly responding to each cry or by surrendering to your impulse to cuddle and comfort.

Through Childhood

As children begin to grow, understand what's going on, and communicate their thoughts, parents play a critical role in shaping their moral and emotional development. Here are the ways in which your

SECRETS FROM RESEARCH
TV Before Two

Many well-meaning parents attempt to enrich their baby's experiential background by sitting him or her in front of a television for daily exposure to a world filled with waving leaves, barnyard animals, humorous clowns, classical music, and the like. But according to the American Academy of Pediatrics, viewing the world on a two-dimensional flat screen does not have a positive impact on a child's thinking skills. In fact, the academy recommends that children get minimal, if *any*, television before the age of two.[2] The few studies that have been done on the matter show that substituting TV "edutainment" for real-life interactions (such as puppet shows) dramatically reduces the toddler's learning.[3]

actions will affect the happiness of your family while building self-esteem and resiliency in your child.

Model positive life choices. It's true that children watch everything you do, so your actions are far more potent teachers than your words. Some parents live healthy, kind, and thoughtful lives—they are natural role models without even trying. But other parents will need to make a more conscious effort to model desirable habits and attitudes. That might include those of you who have lived a prechild lifestyle built on loud music, all-night drinking, and recreational drug use, or more innocent pleasures, such as eating rich foods or riding your bicycle without a helmet. Knowing that your kids learn from your example can definitely put a damper on your wild side.

Fun aside, if you or your co-parent suffer from alcohol or drug abuse, habitual gambling, pornography addiction, or any other compulsive or destructive behavior, get help—from a professional if need be—now! Kids give parents that absolutely best reason to kick the habit. They need you to be healthy and mentally stable.

Respond with love and support. Children's lives can be a tumultuous journey of daily ups and downs. Win the race today—lose a friend tomorrow. Feel proud and confident on Monday—feel embarrassed and scared on Tuesday. Through all these life experiences, our children look to us to gauge their value and worth. How do you respond this important task?

Even if your children's accomplishments don't quite measure up to your expectations, or if you are tempted to tease them for just falling short of what you did at their age, you should hold back the trash talk and be generous in your praise and encouragement. Emotional distance, sarcasm, and criticism for life events can have a strong negative impact on the way a child views himself or herself. It's tough for kids to build a sense of self-esteem when they perceive (rightly or wrongly) that their parents think they're nothing special.

Help children learn coping strategies. Because life can seem like one long series of getting knocked down and then getting back up again, the way you respond to the down times in your child's life will give him or her resiliency skills. In Secret 7, we'll go into this subject of resiliency in more detail, and we'll see that the happiest people are those who have experienced stress and learned to deal with it in constructive ways. But on this subject of parenting right now, what can a parent say to the wannabe actor who gets a bit part in the chorus? Or to the benchwarmer with dreams of hitting home runs?

These life events offer the wonderful opportunity to teach our children the intellectual processes that go into solving problems. They offer parents and caregivers opportunities to show children how and why other people (including us) can't always resolve their upsets for them. But by being proactive, children can find ways within themselves to conquer their fears and failures. Without providing solutions, ask your children to brainstorm some ideas. Didn't make the team this year? Hmm. What can you do? Coax your child to come up with options: maybe try out for a different team closer to your ability level; maybe take lessons so that you'll improve and then try out again later; maybe turn your attention to a different activity where you have stronger skills; maybe form your own team.

There is no easy solution to the pains of childhood dilemmas, but all children need to learn that although life doesn't owe them happiness, it's there for them to pursue.

In the Teens

As children move into the teen years, the challenges of parenting increase. The task of balancing your desire to prepare your offspring for adulthood with their hormonal and biological drive to pull away from you requires a boatload of wisdom, humor, and love.

Happy families know they have influence. In this developmental phase, children are very susceptible to outside influences, including peer groups. In fact, there has been a fair amount of media hype around the research finding that peers influence adolescents more than their parents do. The facts are more complicated than the headlines would lead you to believe. Yes, when it comes to substance abuse, the kids who surround your kids do have an influence. But when it comes to basic values and big decisions (such as the value of honesty and the decision of a college choice), you have greater influence on your children than their friends do.[4]

In fact, a study called "Parent-Teen Relationships and Interactions" examined the level of parental influence on teens and reported these interesting results:[5]

- More than four in five adolescents agreed or strongly agreed that they think highly of their mothers and fathers.

- More than one-half agreed or strongly agreed that they wanted to be like their mother, and slightly under two-thirds agreed or strongly agreed that they wanted to be like their fathers.

- More than three-quarters reported that they really
  enjoy spending time with their mothers or fathers.

Happy families take charge. Even though your teen may suggest that your opinions don't matter, they do. Happy families know this, and the parents feel comfortable taking charge. They don't worry that saying no will make their children unhappy. ("No, you can't wear that outfit to school.") They don't back down from tough decisions because "everyone else it is doing it." (No, you can't spend the weekend camping in the woods with your friends.) They're the parents. They know what's best. They clearly state their expectations, and they live what they preach. This is vitally important in the teen years, when our children are quite sure they know everything there is to know about everything—yet deep down crave parental help and direction. Mark Twain commented accurately on the situation with his usual wit when he said, "When I was a boy of fourteen, my father was so ignorant I could hardly stand to have the old man around. But when I got to be twenty-one, I was astonished at how much he had learned."

I've seen many families who did not understand their children's need for parental authority and, as their children age, find themselves overpowered by out-of-control teenagers. The children I'm talking about here were the ones who got the best of everything and for whom no effort was withheld to ensure their comfort. These children got the message that everything that happened in their families revolved around them.

In her book *The Blessing of the Skinned Knee*, child therapist Wendy Mogel points out, "In their eagerness to do right by their children, parents . . . spoil them emotionally—they overvalue their children's need for self-expression and turn their households into little democracies. [This] does not give their children a sense of self-esteem. Instead, it frightens them by sending the message that their parents are not firmly in charge. By refusing to be authority figures, these parents don't empower their children, they make them insecure."[6] Mogel reminds us of the biblical view of the adult's role in raising children: "Not to make them feel good, but to make them into good people."

Striking the perfect balance in raising teenagers is a nearly impossible feat. But laying out a persistent theme of respect for parents, family values, and self while giving your teen the tools to learn about the world in a healthy, safe, and open environment will pave the way to a happier family.

Adult Children

There's ample advice available for new parents that guide them through the infant, toddler, early childhood, and teen and adolescent years; books, magazines, research studies, and the like abound. But there's little help to be found once those tikes grow into adulthood. In fact, my coauthor, Theresa, has written one of the few books on the subject: *How to Talk to Your Adult Children About Really Important Things*. Theresa wrote this book because the need for guidelines doesn't end with high school or even with college graduation. As children shift into adulthood, the process of achieving independence is often delayed because of college, graduate school, and, of course, months or even years of "just figuring out what I want to do with my life." The secrets of happy families can seem very enigmatic as families struggle with emerging adult children who move back into the home and resume hanging around with their friends and eating out of the refrigerator.

I've dealt with many clients who confront the challenges of having "boomerang kids" in their home. Just at the moment that they anticipate settling into their empty nest for some serenity, their children knock on the door with their belongings in tow. These adult kids are not dumb; they have found the comforts and economic

SECRETS FROM RESEARCH
A Nation of Wimps

The book title *A Nation of Wimps* may sound a bit negative and harsh, but there's no denying that kids today are dragging their feet into adulthood. Using the classic benchmarks of adulthood—leaving home, finishing school, getting a job, getting married, and having children—it has been found that 65 percent of males had reached adulthood by the age of thirty in 1960. By contrast, in 2000, only 31 percent had.[7] Ouch!

benefits of home too appealing to turn down. In some ways, this return can enrich the family; adult children bring new adult perspectives, wild tales of adventure, and stories of all kinds of romantic drama to the dinner table. It may be nice for the parental units, but there is a risk that such arrangements postpone a child's transition into adulthood.

Things don't always go smoothly when adult children reenter the homestead. Your returning brood may object to household rules, such as the need to make the bed or take out the garbage. They may also balk at the very appropriate demand that they pay room and board. Often parents lose sight of a key fact: after a child reaches the age of eighteen, he or she is a legal adult; parents no longer have any obligation to provide hearth and home to him or her. That doesn't mean that the only approach to take with adult children is "My way or the highway"; as you would with your kids at any age, you should take the time to hear why your children seek flexibility on your part. But if you can't agree to disagree, then you're the boss, and, even though it may break your heart to see them take to the highway, it could the first step to entering adulthood. And if you think about it, helping your kids make it into adulthood is what it's all about.

Grandchildren

Many parents end up housing not only their own adult children who come back to roost but also the little chickies of those children as well. For many, this isn't a bad situation. There's a boatload of truth in the adage that it's more fun being a grandparent than a parent. In some ways, being an on-duty grandparent is the best of all possible worlds: watch the kids grow up under your eyes, spoil them rotten, and leave the tough disciplinary stuff to their legal guardians.

Still, even in this secondary role, grandparents can have a profound effect on the lives of children and their levels of happiness in the family. A 2008 British study, the first of its kind, sought to determine if grandparents who help raise grandchildren contribute to a child's well-being. The researchers found that almost one-third of grandmothers regularly cared for their teenage grandchildren, and about 40 percent occasionally helped out. The survey found that grandparents enriched the lives of these teenagers by helping them solve problems and by being there in times of family stress.[8] The more involved grandparents were, the more enriched the children! And we all know that happy children make a happy home.

There is no one hard-and-fast rule for raising children. If there were, then surely we would all be applying the rule, and we'd all have perfect family dynamics! The reality is that the way you raise children (whatever their age) is an amalgam of your own childhood experiences, your cultural values, and the personalities of your children. The one unifying principle is that if children are raised with guidelines similar to those shared by happy families throughout this book, there's a good chance they will continue throughout the course of their lives to contribute to strong and happy family structures. The core values, the entrenched habits of commitment and communication, and the establishment of family and community support all work synergistically to build a strong foundation on which a family builds its identity. These are the building blocks for the security and comfort children need to contribute to the vitality and happiness of the family unit.

DISCIPLINE WISELY

Let's talk about discipline. We all have an idea of how we'd like to see our children behave and develop, yet I see so many parents in my practice who lament the direction that their children are going. They say, "The kids just don't act the way that I envisioned they would." And what was this vision?

What do people want from their children? In my online Happy Family Survey, I asked a lot of questions, but for the one question specifically about raising children, I asked respondents to endorse only one of these statements:

1. Children should strictly follow the rules and regulations set up by their parents.
2. Children should be encouraged to question authority to promote independent thinking, even if it means they challenge their parents.
3. Neither of the above.

What the survey showed was that almost one in four people felt that children should follow a strict code of discipline. Almost 40 percent of the respondents felt that children should not be held to strict guidelines of behavior, but another 40 percent believed that neither description was on the money. Many people who responded to the question—particularly the ones who chose "Neither of the above"—jumped down to the comment section and offered such insights as these:

> "Children should follow rules and expectations set up by parents but be allowed to question as age appropriate. In the end, the parents have the final say."

"Children should generally follow rules and guidelines set by parents, teachers, etc., but should feel free to intelligently discuss emotions/reasons for disagreeing with those expectations."

"We believe there is a middle ground that involves both independent thinking and respectful behavior."

On a simple A, B, or C question, 475 people wrote in to describe their approach to rule setting in their households. Survey respondents clearly had strong beliefs on this issue. Whether they thought that children should strictly follow rules or that children should be free to challenge their parents, most agreed on one thing: the best approach to discipline is a balance of the two.

That's what I would have said too—but far better to hear it from other parents who learned this lesson through trial and error and came out the other side defining themselves as happy family members. Now the task is to find that balance between demanding obedience and allowing independent thought.

———————

We've all heard parents and teachers complain, "The kids are just so out of control; I don't know what to do anymore. I've punished them and taken away just about everything I can, but they still act up all the time."

We hear this statement so often because many people believe that the way to "control" children is through punishment—and that is a big mistake. Discipline is not synonymous with punishment; rather, it is a means of teaching a pattern of behavior and self-control that provides for the moral and emotional growth of children. That's a far cry from "getting out the whip." I'm not a fan of physically hurting children to change their behavior, unless you need to rescue them immediately from a source of harm (such as slapping a child's hand as he reaches for a rattlesnake). Aside from being cruel to the child, hitting just doesn't work. I've spoken to hundreds of parents who spank, slap, push, or otherwise use corporal punishment

---

Secrets of Happy Families

A Balance of Rules and Freedom

Children should have boundaries, but they should also have the freedom to sometimes test their limits. We learn best through experience. If we shelter our children too much, they will enter a world for which they are unprepared. Give them rules to teach them right from wrong, and give them the freedom to learn from their mistakes in a safe environment.

—*Rebecca, 24, married 8 months, no children*

---

as a method of discipline. Although some of them say it gets their kids to alter their behavior temporarily, the vast majority are frustrated by the lack of response in their kids over the long run.

Actually, all forms of punishment (such as grounding, withholding, or yelling) tend to have little effect on a child's behavior over time if they are the only methods of discipline used. An approach that's built on consistency, natural consequences, unity, and love reduces the need for punishment and gives kids the tools they need to understand their boundaries and control their own behavior.

Discipline with Consistency

Consistency in discipline is a must. I can't emphasize this enough, but I'm going to try by sharing a story about rats. When I first started my undergraduate studies at Brown University, I wanted to be a psychology major. But after taking only one course in psychology, I changed my mind because of two factors: statistics and rats.

The statistics part is simple to understand. In order to be a psychology major, I needed to take lots of statistics classes. I'm no math whiz; I consider myself more a people person. And although I know that the study of statistics is an important part of the study of human behavior, I just didn't enjoy spending a lot of time doing the math.

The rats are a different story. I took an Intro to Psych class that had a laboratory requirement. Back then, I thought that the mandatory experiments with rats were a complete waste of time. But, as time teaches us, sometimes the lessons that we blow off as stupid are the ones that end up being the most valuable. In any case, thirty years later, one particular rat experiment helps me explain why consistency in discipline is so important.

Each student was assigned a rat in a metal cage. Into each cage jutted a metal lever, about the size of a stick of gum. As the rat wandered around the cage, checking things out, he eventually hit the lever. The clever electronic gadget attached to the lever then released a tasty rat pellet into the cage. The rat devoured the pellet, and in a very short time he learned that if he hit the lever again, another pellet would appear. Hit lever, pellet appeared. Hit lever again, pellet plopped down the chute again. He pressed the lever at a nice steady rate, and life was good for Mr. Rat.

Then the experiment changed. Instead of giving a pellet to the rat every single time, the rat was now given a pellet every once in a while. This is called variable reinforcement. Sometimes it took three hits; sometimes it took thirteen. You would think that our furry friend would give up at this point, as our little experiment had become work for him. Quite the contrary. Instead of hitting the lever fewer times, the rat began tapping it like mad. His rat mind figured that hitting the lever would eventually result in a pellet, so he became the little rodent-engine that could—tap, tap, tapping until his treat showed up.

Then came the third part of the experiment, called extinguishing. Now that the rat had learned that if he just kept trying, he would get a pellet, we wanted to see if he would stop his lever pushing if we stopped giving him rewards. True to form, he pushed like crazy, but got no pellets at all. Then he took a break, sniffed around

SECRETS FROM RESEARCH
Discipline for Boys

Researchers are beginning to understand that some behavioral problems are rooted in the fact that boys and girls don't learn in the same way. You have to ask what took them so long; parents and teachers have known this since the beginning of time. Michael Gurian, coauthor of *The Minds of Boys*, has long championed an individualized approach to educating children, recognizing that boys tend to be more kinesthetic ("hands-on") learners. Asking an average schoolboy to sit quietly in a seat for forty-five minutes at a time may not be the best way to educate him and may be asking for trouble. Because a boy tends to be less able to tolerate classroom restrictions, and because there may be a delay in the development of his reading and speech abilities compared to girls, he is more prone to be labeled as having learning or behavioral problems. Sometimes, changing the teaching approach is all that's necessary to correct his "disability."[9]

the cage a little, reoriented himself, and pushed again. He returned again and again and, over time, finally stopped trying. Some part of his rat brain said, "My source of pellets has dried up, and it's pointless to push anymore." That's about the sum of what the rat learned, but as a psychology student, I was supposed to learn a bit more.

I don't think I appreciated the full import of the experiment until I had children: if you want someone to do something, then give him or her a reward, and if you want someone to stop doing something, withhold any rewards. Pretty simple.

But there's another more subtle finding from these rat labs: if you want someone to stop doing something, but you withhold rewards *only some of the time* and not absolutely *all the time*, then that person will actually do the behavior *more*, not less.

I saw this lesson in action just the other day in a supermarket. A father and young daughter (about age three) were in the checkout line. Shockingly, there was candy in the very same aisle (what are the chances of that?). So the first thing the little miss did when she got into the aisle was to reach for some candy. I thought to myself, this is like the first part of the rat experiment: when the little girl grabs the candy, it's like a rat pushing the lever. She wants to know whether she'll be rewarded with a treat.

Her father gently took the candy out of her hand and told her that they were not there to buy sweets. The daughter got a bit fussy, reddened a little, and then gave a low-pitched moan. She looked up from her seat in the shopping cart and said, "Please, Daddy, just one!"

Her father again said no and tried to get her to calm down by, creatively, asking her to calm down. Nope, she wasn't about to give in on this one, so she started saying "pleeeease" over and over again. This was like either the second or the third part of the rat experiment. If she pushed her father's "lever" enough, would she be rewarded? The father finally wore down and sternly looked at his little girl and said, "Okay, I'll get you the Lik'm'aid, but just this once. The next time I say no, the answer's no."

If my psychology professor was right, and I believe he was, this father has taught his daughter to cry and whine *more* next time, not less. He thought he was setting a limit; after all, he said "No candy for you!" But his actions spoke louder than his words. As the rat is taught in the second experiment, if you push long enough, eventually something will happen. And each time something does happen, the rat learns to push with more relentless gusto. The next time this father-daughter team is out shopping, do you think the little tike will say to herself, "My dad said last time that I wasn't to whine anymore, so I'll sit quietly and not ask for a thing"? Never! This father has taught her that if she complains enough, she gets what she wants. Not right away, but eventually, so keep on fussing!

Now suppose that instead of variable reinforcement, this kid's dad had tried extinguishing her behavior. In that case, no matter what she said or did, how she moaned or screamed, he would have said, "When I say no, I mean no. No candy." More than likely she'd yell, moan, and scream even louder for a while, just as the rat pushed even more ferociously on the lever. But, like the rat whose supply of pellets had dried up, the little girl would realize that there was no reward in fussing. After a while, the fussing stops. That's the power of consistency.

Supplying this consistency is the parents' job—and don't expect any help from your kids on this. One need only watch a few episodes of the TV shows *Supernanny* or *Nanny 911* to see how fixing problems in children's behavior starts (and ends!) with fixing the behavior of the parents. The fact that a rule makes your child unhappy or frustrated does not make you a bad parent. If you're sure your rules are fair, then stand firm. Temporary unpopularity with your children is the price you sometimes have to pay for being a good parent.

Stay Open to Negotiation

Although I do believe that parents must set firm rules and stand their ground, I also believe that some rules should be negotiable as the children grow. If children are to learn how to shape belief systems that are meaningful to them, then they must have a strong sense of self and the ability to make good decisions. They develop these by observing, questioning, and challenging. And that's a good thing.

Here's how this works. You tell your child to do something. He or she says it's not a good idea. You might say, "Okay, state your case. Why is it not a good idea?" When your child finishes explaining, you may say, "You have an interesting point of view, but do it anyway!" But at least you listened. You showed that you were open to the idea that just because it's your way, it may not always be right. Or, you may say, "You're right. Don't do that this time, and we'll see what happens."

Let's say, for example, that you tell your child that under no circumstances can she ski down a slope by herself at age eleven. (Yes, this is another Haltzman family moment.) Then she points out to you that several other children of that age are skiing alone, and introduces you to parents who let their ten-year-old ski alone. As it is, she's already a much better skier than you are. Is it really worth sticking by your guns on this one, and dragging you and her down for the whole ski day?

In this case, your daughter has taught you something new, and, as you think about it, you realize that when you were in sixth grade you were skiing alone also. Yeah, it means taking a chance that she could become injured without you there, and, yeah, it means giving in on a rule that you made. But sometimes rules need to change and bend and be renegotiated.

Don't misinterpret this to mean that I think children should be the prime movers and shakers in the household hierarchy. They should not. But their opinions and their points of view do matter, and they should know that you are open to changing the rules when they can present a logical and reasonable argument. That's how families can maintain that delicate balance between standing firm and encouraging independent thought.

Discipline with Natural Consequences

Operant conditioning teaches us a lot about how to change behaviors. And in case you haven't figured it out by now, I'm a big fan of consistency. Rewarding good behaviors (such as taking a child to play miniature golf after he or she spends the morning helping Dad clean out the storage bin) is the hallmark of moving someone in the right direction. But often the best education can be gained by making mistakes. Sometimes parents work overtime in an effort to shield children from bad consequences; however, preventing children from seeing the results of their actions can interfere with their learning important life lessons.

For example, Glenna came to my office frustrated with the progress of her fifth-grade son, Jason, who refused to get up in time to get to school in the morning. "I've tried every trick in the book,"

Secrets of Happy Families

They Know When to Negotiate and When to Pay the Consequence

We encourage discussion about rules. But when a rule is broken, consequences are enforced. Our three kids know the rules ahead of time, so they know when they have broken them. They also know that that is not the time to try and negotiate the rules. They must "pay the consequence" and at a later time can discuss changing the rule. And sometimes, their reasoning is sound, and the rule is changed—but not in the heat of the moment.

—*Elle, 38, married 16 years*

---

she stated, "including attempts to reward him with Yu-Gi-Oh! cards and threats of taking away his computer or canceling his weekend scouts' camping trip."

"So what happens," I asked Glenna, "when he doesn't get dressed in time?"

"Thank goodness, that's never happened!" she assured me. "Sometimes I have to dress him because he moves so slowly; other times he misses the bus, and I have to drive him to school. But so far, he's always made it."

Good for Jason, not so good for Glenna. Although Glenna may feel that she is teaching Jason how to pull himself together in the morning, what's really happening here is that Jason is teaching Glenna how best to serve *him*.

To correct Jason's errant ways, I recommended that Glenna start using what are called natural consequences. As the name of the technique implies, the consequences of undesirable behavior will follow naturally as a result of what your child does or doesn't do.

This approach to discipline starts with making expectations clear. To say "I want cooperation" is too vague. I told her that at bedtime, she should clearly state her expectation: "When I wake you tomorrow morning, I want you up and out of bed without any argument or delay, and I expect you to get dressed and be downstairs in fifteen minutes."

Then she should point out the natural consequence if Jason does not meet this expectation: "If you do not get out of bed, I will not nag you, but I will not rush you to the bus or drive you to school. If you don't make the bus, you will walk to school. I'll call the school and tell them you are late, but I won't make an excuse for you. If the school gives you a detention, you'll take it. And if there's any extra work to do from the classes that you miss, you'll be expected to make that up." Now *that* will put a crimp in his day. Glenna may further want to point out, "If you can't get up in time for the morning, that tells me that your mind isn't settled enough to sleep well at night, so all the electronic devices, phones, e-mail, and texts will be shut off at 8 P.M." Then Glenna should make sure that Jason is clear on this plan of action: "Any questions?"

Helping children understand rules and consequences is another way to develop their independent thinking. When possible, family rules should be set before possible conflicts happen: "I am not buying you candy at the checkout counter, so do not ask, whine, or cry when we get there." Then, even young children can be involved in creating rewards and consequences for their actions. As a parent you can ask your child, "If you behave and don't whine for candy, what do you think should be your reward?" No, sorry, a trip to Disney World is not a reward, nor, unfortunately, is a piece of candy from the candy aisle! But you can guide your child to choose a logical consequence, such as "We can stop and feed the ducks on the way home." Okay, deal!

Now, continue to engage your child to take responsibility for his or her actions: "And what should be the consequence if you *do* cry for candy?" Hmm . . . "I don't get the candy and I don't get to feed the ducks?" Good plan.

The idea of consistently enforcing natural consequences extends even beyond family rules. If your teenage daughter is rude to her girlfriend, then she has to experience the sadness of their rift, without your helping soften the blow. If your son forgets to bring money for the school trip, then he doesn't go. Kids who are raised to take responsibility for their own actions grow to be teens and young adults who take the reins of their own fate.

Of course, there are certain cases in which suffering natural consequences doesn't make a whole lot of sense. It's not cool to let your kids go out boating without life vests just so they can see what might happen, and they shouldn't learn the consequences of setting fire to your living room furniture. When it comes to your children's safety or the safety of others, you must intervene and provide mandatory guidelines. There's no room for negotiation there.

Discipline with Unity

If you live in a household with at least two parental figures, there are likely to be great differences in how these adults view discipline. Suppose, for example, two siblings are fighting. One parent says, "Let them fight it out," and the other yells upstairs, "Stop that right now!" Who's right? Although occasionally there are clear-cut "intervene" and "don't intervene" situations, there's no single absolutely right solution. If I could offer one, I'd be in line to win the Nobel peace prize.

Anyone who has children will not be surprised to learn that child rearing is one of the main topics of parental dispute. But parents who are able to keep their kids in line are the ones who know that they won't always agree, and also know what to do when they don't agree.

I'm not shooting for a Nobel prize because I know I don't have all the answers to the problems surrounding discipline, but I do know certain basic rules about parental unity that are bound to help your kids understand how you expect them to behave.

1. Parents must agree on some fundamental rules for the household related to safety and respect for others' comfort and conveni-

ence. There are some households that believe children can drink alcohol in the home (a very common phenomenon among first-generation European American families); others forbid alcohol in any form. There are some households in which the trappings of "please" and "thank you" aren't important; in others they are paramount. Figure out what fits your family's identity, make the rules clear, and stick by them. This may take some compromise, but it's better to get these basic rules set before your children start setting them for you.

2. Adults must reach an understanding of how their individual values influence their parenting. When I was a child, I accidentally broke my sister's nose on a doorknob as I slammed the door on her during a chase. Consequently, I absolutely will allow no door slamming during chases, even if it's in play. However, if my children want to slam a door in protest because they are angry at me, then I don't object as much. My wife, in contrast, doesn't care much about door slamming during play, but grew up in a household raised by a German father, where children were never allowed to show disrespect. She strongly objects to doors slammed in protest.

That was the issue in our house, and when it comes to hot-button issues in your own house, you'll probably have to sit down and talk about your differences, and more than once. The best time to talk is not when you're in the middle of a heated disciplinary issue, but later, when things have calmed down. The key is to respect where your partner is coming from and to try to work within a set of rules in which everyone's needs are taken into account. In our household, the problem was easily solved: no one's allowed to slam doors for any reason!

3. Each parent must show strong public support for the partner, or at least not sabotage the other in front of the children. If two women are raising a young man, and one woman insists that his room be spotless before he goes out, it doesn't mean that her partner is expected to march upstairs and inspect the room with a white glove. But neither should her mate say, within earshot of their son,

"Leave him alone; his room is clean enough!" After he goes off for his tennis match, then the two moms can talk about household cleanliness standards.

4. Play to your strengths. If one adult is better at academics, then the other should permit him or her to have the say over all things educational. If one adult has more fashion (or bargain) sense, then that adult should take the lead when it's time to buy clothes. Nonexperts should still have a say, of course, but must respect the expertise of the other. Remember, just because you have an opinion doesn't mean you are right. You have to accept that there are a lot of good, healthy ways to raise children, and they won't always be your way.

5. Fighting should be private. Of course, sometimes you and your mate will get snippy, and it's important for children to see that when you disagree, you can come back to each other in loving ways. But children exposed to constant bickering actually show a decreased ability to form friendships, a reduction in the quality of schoolwork, and an increased risk for illnesses.[10]

Just at the very moment that I concluded the preceding point, I called my daughter on her cell phone to check in on her. She is only upstairs, but in a truly twenty-first-century circumstance, it was easier to call her on her cell phone than to yell up to her. Alena is seventeen, and she just got back from working the evening shift at the Providence Place Mall. She asked if there was anything to eat; I told her there were leftovers in the fridge. She then asked, "Can you heat it up for me?" Decision time! Do I stop what I'm doing (writing a book) and fulfill my only daughter's simple request? Or do I tell her to come downstairs (and interrupt her IM-ing and texting her friends) and heat up her own darn stir-fry?

You may read this and say, "It's a no-brainer, Dr. Scott; tell her to heat it up herself!" But it's not so simple. It's the weekend, and I don't see as much of my daughter as I'd like, but when she's in her room, it's off-limits to me! Also, I want to reward her for working hard. Moreover, even though I just sat down a few minutes ago to start writing, I feel a little guilty for being self-absorbed. And I enjoy preparing food for her. Now you say, "Well then, it's a no-brainer; just heat it up and enjoy indulging her."

Hold on, there's more. As I prepare to assent to preparing Alena's meal, out of the corner of my eye I see my wife shaking her head no. We've talked about this issue before. We've both observed that our kids need to be more self-sufficient. We've agreed that we will not be so quick to jump to their aid. Issue settled.

"No," I tell Alena, "not tonight." I invite Alena to come down to heat up her own meal.

So far she hasn't come down. And she may not!

You can see that even as my kids prepare to fly the coop, there are still lots of subtleties to raising children. No, nothing's set in stone, even in the Haltzman household, yet there are some basic principles that researchers and those who have contributed to the Happy Family Survey live by, and they are principles that make a lot of sense.

(Update: Alena has come downstairs and now informs me that she doesn't know how to reheat stir-fry. She then says, "Why can't you just help me?" But as she whines about this, she has taken the food out of the refrigerator and put the food in the microwave. And, because we're in the same room, we're actually spending time together, too. It has all worked out for the best, just as my wife knew it would.)

Parents will disagree about many things: whether to help with homework (or not), whether to push a child to write a thank-you note (or not), or whether a child should find a job (or not). They will argue over the benefits and dangers of strict versus lax parenting styles. Moreover, as we'll see in Secret 5, issues surrounding discipline can be particularly dicey in blended families because the non-biological adult in the household may have his or her authority challenged—either by the child or his or her partner. In all these cases, it's important to establish the roles of all the adults involved and to make sure that they are expressed clearly to the children.

GIVE AND TAKE

When our children were younger, we subscribed to *Parents* magazine. Like most topical monthlies, *Parents* had a number of feature articles that did or did not apply to our family. In every edition, they had a section dedicated to specific age groups, and I would flip the pages directly to the section that related to my children. I wanted to learn, learn, learn from experts about how children are and how they are not. But as my children now have grown old enough to start their college careers, I'm struck by a profound truth: raising kids taught me a lot about not only my children but also myself.

In the physical and philosophical world, the insights of children can illuminate our lives. When they ask why you can't get along with your brother, you may be forced to rethink a long-standing feud. When they ask why we can't just take our Razor scooters to the store instead of driving, you may suddenly realize that what you thought of as a chore can be a bonding experience. They may challenge your perceptions of God by asking questions about a pet's death or life on other planets. They might observe (more intimately than anyone else is permitted to) how you and your mate interact, and they will ask why you raise your voice or turn red in the face when you argue. They do pay attention! Once you have children, life will never be the same. Their questions, their needs, their very existence change everything about a family. And that's a good thing.

Expect and accept that children expand your family, and you'll find life oh-so-much happier and your family much closer. This is true no matter what the shape of your family. But if you're a blended family, the next chapter's additional tips for handling a mixed bag of kids are specifically for you.

Happy Families...
Blend

"Sometimes it's like a circus in my house," says Audrey, a thirty-seven-year-old woman who sits next to her husband, Brian, on my office couch. "Brian introduced himself to me at a grade school function, so I knew he was a dad when I met him. He divorced his wife because she was addicted to drugs, and then he gained custody of his two children three years ago. I had never been married, but I had two children from another relationship. When Brian and I decided to get hitched, it didn't feel like my family increased by three; it felt like it increased by three hundred!"

Audrey took pride in her new family, and, even though she thought she had had a good handle on how to have a happy family before she met Brian, there was something so different in the shape of her new arrangement that it seemed that all the rules had changed.

"To be honest, Dr. Scott," she told me, "I thought that things would fall into place easily, but it took a lot of effort to get my family and his family to work together as one team."

Getting any newly formed family to work together as a team takes time and effort. That's to be expected when people from different backgrounds and upbringings choose to live under the same roof. And blended families take this "bringing together" to a whole new level.

This chapter on blended families offers many insights that are pertinent to every family, but it is addressed directly to those of you who are working hard to make all the pieces of your blended family fit together in harmony. The rest of you can flip the pages over to Secret 6, which is about conflict. Now *that's* a topic that pertains to all of us!

WHAT IS A BLENDED FAMILY?

A textbook definition of a blended family might say that it's a family composed of *two individuals who have offspring who are not blood-related to one or both of their parents*. But this simple definition belies the complexity of this family structure, which can take many forms. On the basis of my experience with families of all shapes and sizes, I divide the blended family category into five groups:

1. Open-Adoption Families

When families adopt children into their home and the birth parents and grandparents continue to be involved in the lives of their biological children, a blended family is created.

This can become pretty complicated. For example, I have to admit I was a bit confused when I met Ashley, who at eighteen came to see me in my Rhode Island office for a medication evaluation. Ashley introduced me to her mother, Elaine, who sat in the chair next to her. Yet in describing her weekend, she talked about her plans to visit her siblings and "other mom" in nearby Massachusetts. I guess Elaine could see the quizzical expression on my face, so she interrupted Ashley to explain: "I adopted Ashley when she was nine months old because her mom voluntarily gave up parental rights to me."

Elaine had been unable to have children. She knew Ashley's biological family, and jumped at the chance to adopt Ashley and raise her as her own. Because Ashley's biological mother chose to maintain contact with Ashley, they have had a connection throughout the course of Ashley's life.

In blended families such as Ashley's, there are varying degrees of contact between the child and the birth family. In some instances, contact is limited to letters and e-mails; in other cases,

Secrets of Happy Families

This Is Our Family:
Perhaps Unconventional But Definitely Wonderful

My husband and I were lucky to be present at the birth of both of our children, who we then adopted. (I was even the birth coach for my son's birthmother.) Even now when my son is sixteen years old and my daughter is twelve, I really value having their birthmothers—both amazing women—in our lives. They are certainly a part of what we call our family.

No doubt an open adoption leads to some interesting situations. When my daughter's birthmother was pregnant, I introduced her to my son's birthmother, and they became good friends. In fact, when my daughter's birthmother got married, my son's birthmother was her bridesmaid and my then-four-year-old daughter was her flower girl. This collection of interrelated people was nothing new to any of us. Every year around Christmas, we invite both extended birth families (reaching even to great-birthgrandparents) to our house. This is our family. My daughter wrote a wonderful school paper about how she treasures this family ritual. We're all friends; over time and with work on communication and openness, we've become very comfortable together, and I think that's a gift to our kids. I'm glad my children know their birth families and embrace them.

From my point of view as the parent, I like the open adoption because it allows me to know so much about my children: who they are and where they came from. The only downside is that in an open adoption, you can never forget the pain the birth family goes through. You see it up close, and you can't pretend this was an easy choice. But this is also a constant and powerful reminder of how brave the birthmother has been and how special the child is.

Some people may call our family "unconventional," but to us it's just who we are, and we're happy with it.

—Diane, 52, married 22 years

members of the extended birth family are involved in many aspects of daily life and are certain to be a part of birthdays, holidays, and other celebrations.

It's easy to understand why such an arrangement can be a complicated, emotional experience for adults and children. In most cases, the legal question is clear (although in some cases, a child is informally raised by another family member with no legal arrangement). But documentation and official state seals can't legislate emotions. For an adult who is raising a child who is still attached to another (biological) parent, landmark events—from the first step to the first prom date—may involve emotions that other parents don't deal with: resentment at having to share the moment, magnanimity at being able to play a part in two (or more) people's lives. Adults who give their children over to others to raise may experience anything from gratitude to jealousy.

As children move into their adolescence, they too can experience a range of conflicting emotions as they begin to explore identity issues. My clinical experience is that at some point almost all children, not just adopted ones, believe that some terrible cosmic mistake was made, and they don't belong in their families. That's a normal part of being a teenager, an important stage for being able to separate and individuate from the family of origin. But when what is a normal emotion for any kid is felt by an adopted child, it can take on special significance. The key to thriving in a blended adoptive family is knowing who's who, setting clear boundaries, and being aware that all kinds of doubts, challenges, and emotional upheavals may follow. It's part of the growth process—and there's nothing like adopting a child to spark that growth—but the rewards can be like nothing else!

2. Foster Families

When a governmental agency (such as child protective services) determines that a child cannot live with his or her biological parents, it assigns that child to live with another family. Once that child crosses the threshold of his or her foster home, he or she creates a blended family.

Jan returned from her eight-hundred-mile journey to Maryland beaming. "I was so proud," she stated, pointing to the special American flag pin on her lapel. Her foster son, Rick, had graduated from the naval academy, and she and her husband were there to soak in his glory. But this bit of revelry was bittersweet; also at Rick's graduation was his caseworker from the foster agency, who also saw Rick as "hers."

Jan and her husband are like a lot of foster parents: when they accept a child into their house, they make him or her their own. In Rick's case, he lived with Jan's family for four years, from ages fourteen to eighteen, and during that time, Jan and her husband helped him through first dates, got him geared up for team sports, picked him up from after-school activities, and brought him to their church. Jan has had other young men stay with her, some for just a week, others for a full year. Each time a boy moves in, he becomes, as far as Jan is concerned, a member of the family—a blended family.

Foster families have a special place in our society. Composed of couples (occasionally individuals) who fill the gap when the biological family unit of a child falls apart, they have the task of

Secrets of Happy Families

Acceptance in Foster Families

What makes foster family work for us is being accepting of each other's differences and celebrating the little successes of getting to know each other during our time together.

—*Mary, 48, married 2 years, with five children (step, biological, and foster)*

providing a safe and loving home for a child. In the midst of doing this generous and important job, foster parents must act like parents. But they are not parents. It sounds easy enough, but all foster parents know that the position is rocked with many emotional ups and downs. Foster homes are hotbeds of diversity and change.

Foster families are unique among blended families for several reasons:

The child is often "hurt" in some way. When a child comes into a foster home, it usually means that something was wrong with the child's home of origin (such as parents who are deceased, incarcerated, abusive, or drug addicted), or it may mean that the child suffers from a medical problem (such as developmental disabilities) that the biological parents cannot manage. When a child is removed from his or her birth home, the hurt doesn't go away when he or she is dropped off at his or her new residence.

The definition of family is always in flux. Usually when a child is removed from the home of origin, the move lasts until the child's parent or parents can pull together the resources to accept the child back. But the child and the parent don't know when, if ever, that moment will be. So it's hard for families to be able to know how to see themselves. As one foster mother I know asks, "If Tabitha comes in September, should we plan to buy Christmas presents for her?" It's more than an academic question, because how long each child stays affects relationships with other children (foster, step, or biological) in the home.

The attachment is ambiguous. When a kid joins a foster family, the family is usually told whether or not the child will be adopted away. Even if the child is not to return home, sometimes adoption agencies forbid (or strongly discourage) adoption by the foster family. So the situation begs the emotional (if not practical) question: What is the adult's relationship to the child, and vice versa? When a child moves from house to house, he or she in effect adds to an ever-growing roster of "family" members. Clearly, it's not possible, or even advisable, to develop close emotional bonds with all of them.

For all these reasons, foster families, more than any other kind of family (blended or not), must exercise one crucial characteristic that will help them through: flexibility. They must start each day saying, "I know who's in my family this morning; I wonder whom it will be composed of tonight?" Through this capacity to tolerate the unknown, foster families also function best when they hold fast to their values and, through it all, keep their humor.

3. Unmarried-Couple Families with Children

When two adults who are emotionally and romantically involved decide to live together, but choose not to marry (or engage in a formal commitment ceremony), they form a blended family if they reside with children who are the products of previous relationships.

Ron and Maria are one such family. Each in their early thirties, they both had children from previous relationships. When Ron's apartment lease was running out, Maria invited him to move in with her and her daughter. Now that Ron is there, he helps pay the rent and occasionally joins Maria and her daughter for outings. When Ron's son comes by, they sometimes make it a foursome. Because they share quarters and expenses, and feel very fond of each other, they see themselves as a family.

Maria tells me, "We're not ready to commit to marriage, though. We're too scared that we'll screw it up."

Like other kinds of blended living arrangements, living in a cohabiting arrangement has its challenges; chief among them is the frequent lack of formal definition of roles among the members of the household. When a child is adopted, he calls his new caregivers "Mom and Dad." When a child is taken in to foster care, she calls them "foster-mom" or "foster-dad." When his parents marry a new partner, it's a "stepparent." However, when two adults decide to live together, the lines of authority can occasionally get fuzzier.

In some cohabiting blended households, children are not expected to consider their parent's "roommate" as co-parent with equal authority. This family dynamic certainly makes the task of blending a tougher one, but over time a tacit understanding about the leadership role of the adults usually develops. In any case, because there is no "official" status of the adult's connection to the child, the boundaries are looser in this arrangement than in any other form of blended family.

In Secret 2, we discussed the higher rates of separation among adults who live together rather than marry. But living together and marrying aren't mutually exclusive; many people who start out living together end up marrying. In fact, many of the clients whom I treat consider living together to be a step toward marriage, sure that it will lead to a better connection if they choose to finally tie the knot. But that's not what the research shows.

Compared to couples who moved in together *after* they made plans to marry, those who cohabited *before* being engaged were the most likely to have difficulties in their relationship both before and after marriage. They also had more dissatisfaction and less confidence about their connection. Moreover, couples who live together before marriage describe themselves more frequently as less committed to the future of the relationship and, when it came to men, less dedicated to their marriages. Ultimately, the research shows that they end up having a higher divorce rate than couples who plan *first* to get married, *then* live together.[1]

Ultimately, the best way to shore up the boundaries and inject a sense of permanence and security in the lives of the children involved is to marry. Short of that, be clear, both to yourself and to your partner, about your level of commitment to each other. Then share it with the children to make sure that everyone knows where everyone else stands.

4. Stepfamilies

This family is formed when at least one of the new partners is already a parent who has remarried after a divorce or death of the other parent in a nuclear family. Best estimates tell us that, based on traditional marriage, about 20 percent of all families fall into this category, and about 25 percent of children will at some point be raised in such a family.[2] The results of my online Happy Family Survey match these national statistics: about 21 percent of all the families who responded describe themselves as having stepchildren in the house.

Claire and Tim are one such couple in the process of creating a blended stepfamily. Tim was forty-seven and had already been divorced twice when he met Claire, herself a divorcée with a twelve-year-old son whom she had been raising alone for eight years. Tim was a music teacher at the local school and was tutoring Claire's son when they met. When I saw them in my office, they were struggling with the adjustment of being a new family—a normal stage of development. But two things were clear: first, Claire loved Tim; second, she was thankful for his masculine presence in the home: "I want this marriage to work, and I want to Tim to be happy; he's a stabilizing force for my son, and that's priceless to me."

Tim concurred. "I wanted to help Claire and her son start a new life with me, and I wanted to do it as her husband."

Both partners had solid motivation for making their marriage work. And that is a great way to begin to build a happy blended family.

5. Gay and Lesbian Families

Partners with children from a prior opposite-sex marriage, through adoption, from surrogates (two men using a woman to carry a child for them), or through sperm donors (two women with outside donation from a friend, sibling, or anonymous donor) create blended families.

While I was doing research for this book, Demian, the director of Partners Task Force for Gay and Lesbian Couples (find more information at www.BuddyBuddy.com), gave me some useful insights; one was that virtually all families of same-sex partners and children he works with see themselves as blended. He said, "Same-sex couples that have children do so by previous marriages, by adoption, and sometimes via a surrogate. In all these circumstances, they deliberately create a blended family."

Lyanne, Maura, and their three children are such a family. Thanks to anonymous donor sperm, Maura gave birth to their two girls (now ages seven and two), and Lyanne gave birth to their son (now age four). "In our situation," says Lyanne, "there are no 'accidental' children. We made a very conscious decision to be a family, and we are extremely happy with that decision."

Perhaps one of the reasons this blended family feels such happiness is that Maura and Lyanne have made an effort to expose the children to all types of families: the ones with a mom and a dad, the ones with two moms or two dads, the ones with just one mom, and so on. "The kids don't have any sense of being 'different,'" Lyanne says. "In fact, our son loves announcing to anyone who will listen that he has two moms."

However, as Lyanne is quick to point out, "One of the big reasons that we haven't experienced any family problems around our family structure is that we live in a place that is open and accepting of our family. I imagine if we lived in a less accepting part of the country our situation would be very, very different."

Their story highlights the universal truth that all families are a product of their society, and it reminds us that blended gay or lesbian families have unique challenges in how others see them. Unlike Lyanne and Maura, many of the gay and lesbian families I deal with feel as if their position as a family is challenged by some of their straight neighbors, who may pose hurtful questions, such as, "Which one is the father [or mother]?" Because gay and lesbian families don't fall into easily defined categories of gender roles, it may be difficult for nongay families to accept them.

That is a challenge that many gay and lesbian couples are ready to take on as they build their families. As a blended group, they are in good company; as we've seen, the term *blended* applies to many families—adoptive, foster, cohabiting, step, and gay and lesbian.

HOW MANY BLENDED FAMILIES ARE THERE?

It's hard to say exactly how many American families are considered blended. We do know that only about 61 percent of American children live with both their biological mother and father for their first eighteen years of life.[3] We also know that about half of all marriages today involve at least one individual who has been married before, and that about 75 percent of divorced individuals are likely to remarry.[4]

When you consider the number of parents who split and then join homes with another partner, or the number of children who live in adoptive or foster homes, you know there are a lot of blended families out there.

As numerous and as varied as blended families are, they all seem to have something in common. Almost without exception, the comments posted on the Happy Family Survey by these family members reveal a unifying theme: making a blended family work is a challenge!

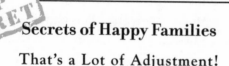

Secrets of Happy Families

That's a Lot of Adjustment!

When our daughter was five, we fostered our two nieces and a nephew who were five, four, and two at the time. We went from a single-child, multi-income family to a multichild, single-income family. It took a lot of adjustment for everyone involved. We kept our sanity by communicating openly, regardless of how we felt. Some days were terrible, some were perfect, but by being honest and sharing our frustrations and our triumphs, we grew into the experience and learned from it.

—*Carrie, 30, married 8 years*

PHASES OF A BLENDED FAMILY

Researchers have found that when individuals from different families come together, it takes some time to form a fully integrated *new* family. Elizabeth Einstein, coauthor of *Strengthening Your Stepfamily*, describes five distinct stages on the way to stepfamily happiness that, in many ways, can be applied to all blended families: (1) hopefulness, (2) confusion, (3) crisis, (4) stability, and (5) commitment.[5] Let's take a look at each one of those five stages individually.

Hopefulness

There's not a soul alive who doesn't understand the hopefulness that wraps its arms around a new family. But when a new family emerges out of the remnants of the old, as it does with blended families, the hopefulness can be even more intense. As Woody Allen once said, "A second marriage is the triumph of hope over experience." This is so true. Whether in a second marriage, in a marriage with adopted or foster children, or in a gay or lesbian relationship, the two adults who choose to build their family from a patchwork of individuals hope that they can form a bond that will last a lifetime. The children are hopeful that their new parent will be a source of comfort, inspiration, and stability. Everyone holds on to very high expectations that there are brighter days ahead.

 SECRETS FROM RESEARCH
Don't Just Hope

First marriages usually end with negative feelings between a couple, and the adults involved often conclude that the relationship was a "bad match." But studies show that second marriages end at rates 10 percent higher than first marriages.[6] In most cases, it's not so much whom you marry as what attitude and skill set you bring to the marriage that will determine whether it lasts or not. I strongly encourage couples who plan to marry, and *especially* ones who plan to remarry, to join marriage education classes. Knowing how to have a good relationship will take you a lot further than being head over heels in love and hoping that love will conquer all.

Confusion

The second phase of blended families emerges soon after the glow of hopefulness wanes. The truth is that new relationships that involve step-, foster, or open-adoption children include a full trunkload of emotional baggage, much of it unresolved, from the previous relationship. And we can't make that past disappear. So when a family blends, there is bound to be confusion about allegiances, responsibilities, and roles.

Some of the most common problems have to do with deciding how to deal with visitation schedules, shared custody, split loyalties, and different house rules. And then there are the problems that surround kids who consciously or unconsciously try to sabotage the new family (perhaps, in stepfamilies of divorce, hoping to bring their parents back together), kids who play one family against the other, and kids who struggle to figure out how their relationship with their new parents differs from the one they have, or had, with their biological parents.

And it's not just the kids who can get confused. Many couples who come into my office are seeking to understand just how the emotional and practical pieces of this puzzle fit together. The feeling of confusion often leads to family upheaval.

Secrets of Happy Families

Time Together

The first major task of our married life was merging a blended family with an eight-year-old and a sixteen-year-old. It was more difficult for the sixteen-year-old because he was used to living with just his dad and without any real responsibilities or expectations. My eight-year-old was disappointed because he was excited about having a big brother, but his new brother was not open to the relationship. We weathered it by making sure Mom and Dad agreed (at least in front of the boys) so they couldn't weaken our authority by claiming "But my dad/mom said I could!" Spending time at home playing games, watching movies, or even doing chores all together has helped us grow as a family and has really helped our older son get to know his younger brother and actually enjoy him.

—*Rachelle, 39, married 4 years*

Crisis

Nearly every blended family goes through a stage of crisis that threatens to disrupt the integrity of the household. I worked closely with a couple, Sandy and Sam, who, through their marriage, brought a teen boy and teen girl from the two different families into the same household. Trouble started almost immediately, but came to the crisis point when Sam's boy, Todd, was a senior in high school. He and some friends secured some beer for a party. Todd invited his stepsister, April, one year younger, to join the party, where she drank so much that she needed to be taken to the hospital to have her stomach pumped.

When the parents learned how the events unfolded, they were, of course, very upset with the children. But Sandy expressed intense

---

Secrets of Happy Families

Getting Help from the Ex

We are a blended family, and as such, have had plenty of difficult circumstances with getting to know each other, like each other, and grow to love each other. My biological daughter (age six) was originally very rude to my husband and was not listening well to him. So I called my ex-husband (her dad) and asked if he and I could have a meeting with my husband and my daughter. That way, my daughter would understand that her dad too felt it was important for her to be respectful of my husband. In the end, she knew we were all on the same page. It really helped.

—*Heather, 32, married 4 years*

---

anger at both her stepson and her second husband. Moreover, April's biological father was the first to the hospital, and he was enraged that his daughter's custodial parents would allow this to happen. What a mess!

Thankfully, April was released from the hospital the same night, but the family issues that came up after this crisis lasted far longer. In fact, this single event was almost enough to drive the new family apart.

But the family rallied and faced the challenges of blending successfully. Sandy and Sam brought both children to counseling, including consultation with a substance abuse specialist. They restricted their children's after-school activities, and actually worked with the police to help track down the liquor store that sold the boys alcohol. While this new family was mounting full-blown damage control in their own home, they also sought to involve the other parents in the community. Working together as a team, but bringing in other important people in their lives, Sandy, Sam, Todd, and April managed to form a united front as a family, grow stronger through the effort, and cultivate a sense of safety and security around each other.

Stability

Sometimes couples don't survive a crisis and choose to dissolve the new union. But often those families that successfully navigate through the white-water rapids of adjustment find quieter waters ahead.

The fourth stage, stability, is one in which members of the family come to understand their roles and begin to define shared values that help them move the family together toward a single goal. This sense of stability is no small thing for those individuals who came to this new family through instability in the family before.

During this stage there will still be arguments, and interruptions and disruptions from the biological parents of the children, but the shared vision of the family members will help keep everyone moving in the right direction—toward the final phase, commitment.

Commitment

Finally (and by finally, I mean that the process can take up to a decade in some cases), the blended family moves to the commitment phase. You might have thought that when two people stand at the altar and take their vows, that would be commitment enough. But this phase of the family goes beyond the vows; this phase is entered into only when the family becomes a unified force—when each member sees each other as an ally in life's endeavors. Knowing that their new mother, father, sister, or brother is there to stand by them at all times helps all family members find the security they need.

Not every blended family reaches this stage, as many foster families recognize that a short-term involvement in a child's life will not establish a lifetime of commitment. And commitment also falters in stepfamilies when the second marriage doesn't last (60 percent divorce, most before seven years of marriage),[7] but when the new family does stay together, it's a force to be reckoned with.

THE PERKS OF COMMITMENT

Every member of a blended family in which a once intact family reshapes itself and joins with another knows that relationships aren't always easy—after all, they've already wrestled with the realities of at least one disappointing experience. But in that first phase of hopefulness, the new family members all put aside their previous irritations and frustrations and looked forward to attaining the rewards of their new commitment. Some of the positives gained by those in a happily blended family are no different than the benefits of any family life: companionship, support, shared values, and lots and lots of love. However, beyond the many blessings that accompany the formation of any happy family, blended families have the unique ability to enjoy positive experiences that traditional nuclear families lack.

For example, a blended family exposes children to a broader range of human interaction. If a child's biological father is a drill sergeant and his new father is more relaxed about chores and schedules, then he will have intimate exposure to the fact that there is more than one way to live one's life. If a child who has been raised in the Jewish faith accompanies her new Methodist stepsiblings to religious services, each has a chance to experience firsthand the differences and similarities among religions.

I grew up with the same siblings and same parents my whole life. But I lived in South America as an exchange student when I was seventeen years old. When I arrived in Bolivia, I called my host parents "Mamá" and "Papá," and their children were considered my siblings. I was new to their culture and attended their church with them, went on their family outings, met their relatives and friends.

Secrets of Happy Families

We Accept Their Choices

Occasionally my stepchildren's biological mom will challenge the kids, when they choose to spend time with their father instead of attending an event with her. In these instances, we (their dad and I) reaffirm our love and support of the children no matter where they choose to spend their time. We have tried diligently to make our home a safe haven free of stress and drama—since we can only control and handle these elements of their lives. As time passes (and the events that are causing the stress pass away), our relationships in our home are strengthened and shored up because we have handled the situations in this way. Being willing to listen nonjudgmentally and supportively has definitely benefited our relationships and communication with our (his) children. I believe our handling of this situation will have lasting benefits as the children move into the upcoming tween/teen years. They have past proof that our love and acceptance of them as persons is not hinged on our feelings about their choices.

—*Keira 37, married 3 years*

I still had my family back home in the good ol' U.S. of A., but I had this family also, and to this day, I think of this sojourn in Bolivia as the most profound life experience I have ever had. For me it was part of personal growth and spiritual development that grew from the chance to be a part of a new culture and a new family.

That's what being in a blended family can offer—all the treasures and life lessons to be found in a cultural exchange.

Beyond the benefits of learning a new lifestyle, there's another bittersweet advantage of being in a blended family, particularly a stepfamily. Because children who live in a blended household are frequently the product of a family that was not able to sustain itself, having them participate in an intact household can provide a model that they can take with them into their own adulthood. Also, if the two parents of this new family can learn how to sustain a long-term committed relationship, then they instill optimism in children about the chances of having a happy marriage themselves, and teach them skills to make marriage work.

For families that had been headed by single parents, being in a blended family may have additional advantages. There are more adults to split the tasks and provide companionship to each other. Heterosexual blended families provide an opportunity for children to be exposed to parents of both genders, and help balance their view of gender roles.

There's another real bonus to surviving and thriving in a blended marriage—bragging rights. Many men and women leave a previous relationship flooded with negative emotions—from embarrassment and guilt to anger and frustration. Discovering how to build a lasting relationship between two adults, especially when you have the additional challenges of balancing the needs of all the new people in your life, gives you every right to feel proud of your accomplishments.

STRATEGIES FOR SUCCESS

Getting it right in a blended family sometimes happens by accident, but don't count on it. The process of combining two separate families into one works best if you have a plan.

Manage Expectations

First be clear about having a realistic sense of what's possible and what isn't in a blended family. Don't expect the Brady Bunch lifestyle after you all move in together. Expect a bumpy road and realize that not knowing exactly what you are doing is par for the course. Ease up on yourself, your mate, and your kids, and enjoy the ride.

Secrets of Happy Families

Successful Adoptions

I'm an older stay-at-home Dad. After we adopted a four-year-old from Asia, we found that the keys to success were (1) communication between parents, (2) workshops, (3) counseling, and (4) talking with other adoptive parents.

—*Jim, 69, married 3 years*

Many newly blended families try to reduce their troubles by building a wall between the "other" families who are involved in the lives of the children. But in most cases that's not a great idea. Unless the biological or stepparents of your (or your step-) children provide an unhealthy environment for children, they should be integrated into the new family unit as extended family members.

I want to be clear here: if you and your former mate (or your child's birth parent) could never get along, or if you felt that your relationship with that person was toxic, that doesn't necessarily mean that the relationship between this person and your child must also be toxic. If you're going to help your child transition between the families, you have to keep a reality check on your negative feelings toward your child's parent (assuming the other parent is mentally, emotionally, and physically capable of continuing a healthy relationship with your child).

Sometimes your new partner can actually help you do that. That's what Tara learned when she moved in with Manny after breaking up with her old boyfriend. Tara swore she'd do everything in her power to keep her four-year-old daughter from that previous relationship away from her ex. "But," said Tara a year later, "Manny really helped me to see that Emily was attached to her dad and he deserved a chance to see her. When we first had the discussion, I was upset with Manny for saying that; I thought that he had taken sides against me. But when I realized that he wasn't threatened by my relationship with Emily's dad, I decided I didn't need to dig in my heels." Today, Manny and Emily's dad continue to get along, and occasionally spend time together. And Tara is comfortable knowing that her daughter (and her newborn son) are surrounded in love.

Build a Loving Home Away from Home

Noncustodial parents also have to work on their branch of the family tree. They may now be remarried or living alone or cohabiting, and have to find a way to make their children feel at ease in this new home. This isn't an easy task.

When children visit the home of the noncustodial parent, there's often a lot of tension. This uneasy feeling probably has its roots in the fact that, although most children in blended families haven't read the textbooks on human psychology, they have an uncanny suspicion that they're not living in an ideal world. And because they have so little control over their lives, they are often filled with fear and insecurity. The child's intense emotional response to transitioning between homes is a sobering reality that both custodial and noncustodial parents have to handle with patience and love.

No matter what life events caused the breakup of one family and the blending of another, children who spend time in the "other home" need special care and attention. It's important for children to feel that the biological parent has a place for them in his or her home—and by extension in the heart. If your son or daughter arrives at your home only to see your collection of last year's sweaters piled on his or her bed, it gives a message that your child is taking up space that you'd rather have for other things.

SECRETS FROM RESEARCH
Who's the Boss?

Disciplining children in a blended family can be a bit tricky. (See Secret 4 for general information on parental discipline.) There's always the question of what role the non–birth parent plays in setting and enforcing the rules. First, recall that the stepparent and the child are new in each other's lives, so there will be a natural evolution of their relationship. Initially, the stepparent may take more of a passive role in disciplining. But, over time, the biological parent must cede authority to the new mate, and the kids had better know it![8]

My rule of thumb is that at the very least, the child should treat the stepparent with the kind of respect that should be afforded a teacher. At the most, a stepparent should have the same degree of the authority, never more, than has the biological parent of the child. Although it may seem convenient for the "pushover" biological parent to cede all disciplinary matters to his or her new, stricter mate, there is a great risk that doing so will set up a pattern of resentment and hostility in the children that may last well into adulthood. If, in contrast, the biological parent is the strict one and the new stepparent is more lenient, it can also strain the family.

The union of two individuals that creates a blended family also creates a new parental team; both parents together need to step up to the plate and work together to set and enforce appropriate limits.

Creating a home away from home for your child means setting up an individual space that is designed to make him or her feel comfortable and at ease in this far-from-ideal situation. With this goal in mind, as the noncustodial parent you should try to establish the following:

1. A sleep area specifically dedicated to the children where they can keep personal items, such as their clothing.

2. Age-appropriate space in the bathroom for toiletries or makeup and hair products.

3. Uncluttered room to study or do homework, stocked with study materials (paper, computer, no. 2 pencils—you get the idea).

4. A storage area or closet for your children's belongings.

5. Designated space to play that has room for books and toys that reflect your child's personal tastes. You don't, however, need to duplicate every item your child has in the other parent's home. If you don't believe in television, video games, or graphic comic books, you don't have to have them in your house. Ensuring consistency between households demands that there be objects that have meaning and entertainment value to your children, but it doesn't mean that each household must have a Wii.

It's not necessary for you to buy a trailer and attach it to your home to meet these criteria; even if you have a foldout bed, a desk that pulls out from under a table, and a basket of special supplies, your children will get the message that they have a home with you.

Of course, the most important element that your children need can't be designed by an architect and can't be bought at IKEA. No matter how the physical setting looks, and no matter what's in it, it must be a real home to your child. And the only ingredient you need for that is your love.

SECRETS FROM RESEARCH
Helping Yourself

Sometimes the struggle to make things fall into place in a blended family is just too difficult to handle alone. The creation of a new and happy family may be thwarted because the pain of the previous relationship is too great or because your own personal issues (such as early childhood trauma or a lack of good modeling of behavior on the part of your parents) interfere with sincere efforts to form a happy blended family. In cases like these, it's often necessary to seek individual counseling to work through your issues. Once you can feel comfortable in your own skin, you'll be better able to help others feel comfortable in theirs.

As you and your family go through the stages of blending, you'll find that keeping this family happy requires forethought, open discussions, and respect for the legal, biological, and emotional bonds that weave their way through all the relationships involved. As in all families, getting it right takes work, but it's well worth it in the end.

Once you've reached that last stage of commitment, you'll find that your little clan is really no different from other traditional families; you'll have great days and not so great days. To prepare for those troublesome times, be sure you turn the page to uncover Secret 6.

Secret 6

Happy Families...
Handle Conflict

Everybody in every family fights sometimes. But not everybody fights fair. I've spent my career studying how families interact, and I can tell you that when it comes to resolving family conflict, I use the five basic Fair Fight Facts:

1. All couples fight.
2. We all need to be heard.
3. We need to treat each other with respect to survive conflict.
4. A hostile start results in a harsh end.
5. The fight must be over by bedtime.

Bringing awareness of these facts into your next family fight (which you certainly are bound to have!) will help you survive, and may actually help your family grow stronger.

FAIR FIGHT FACT 1: ALL COUPLES FIGHT

It's a good bet that you and your mate aren't always in total agreement—and you're in good company. In theory, just about everybody knows that every other married pair dukes it out verbally. Despite this knowledge, many couples often cite the inability to agree on things as one of the primary reasons why they think something's wrong with their relationship. They just never expected arguments to be part of the marriage picture.

I've spoken to many individuals who claim they don't remember their parents *ever* arguing. Other people grew up without parents who lived together, so, although they may have experienced lots of discord, they never got to see how couples resolve disagreement. Those newlyweds who looked to TV or the movies for the 411 on relationships have been misled with images of ideal marriages in short sound bites. Sitcoms and reality TV shows don't show how real relationships work. So how are we, now the heads of our families, supposed to know how to handle conflict in a way that's good for the whole family?

Most Couples Don't Disagree About Everything

Remember the common family values we discussed in Secret 1? Most couples I work with read through that list of values and agree that they share many of the same basic desires.

Here's a brief questionnaire that I'm sure will reinforce the point. Check the statement if it holds true for you, your partner, or both of you:

You   Your Mate

_____   _____   If we have children, I want them to get a good education.

_____   _____   If given a choice to drop everything today and become a missionary in a third-world country, I would say no.

_____   _____   It bothers me when people litter.

_____   _____   I'd like to have more money than I currently have, especially if I could have it without increasing my work hours.

_____   _____   I think our children should be married before they get (or get someone) pregnant.

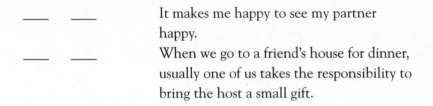

____ ____   It makes me happy to see my partner
happy.

____ ____   When we go to a friend's house for dinner,
usually one of us takes the responsibility to
bring the host a small gift.

How'd you do? How'd your partner do? I could ask a thousand more questions just like those, and in most cases you'd concede that yes, "if you put it that way, we agree on things." You may even see eye-to-eye about more controversial questions, such as whether your children should get body piercing, whether your family should have a religious identity, or whether you should be buried or cremated.

One of the stumbling blocks in building happy families is that we take for granted the things we agree on. In most cases, we really are more alike than different, but we tend to focus more on the differences. Once you make a conscious effort to pay attention to your points of agreement, you'll find it easier to accept the things you don't agree on—you can simply agree to disagree.

Couples Can Agree to Disagree

Now that you can see that you two are in accord on many issues, you've surely put down this book for a moment, jumped into the arms of your mate, and expressed a belief that you two will live together in perfect harmony. Right?

Of course not. I may have demonstrated your similarities in beliefs, goals, and dreams, but unless you're the most easily influenced person in the world, your mind will still want to focus on the things that you don't agree on. In fact, because you're not the most easily influenced person in the world, you can't easily let it go when your partner makes a point that you don't agree with. In fact, he or she is likely to do many things over the course of the day that rankle you. So how do you solve these nasty little problems that come up? Simple. You don't!

Studies show that when couples disagree on a major issue, about three out of four times they don't come to any resolution even half a decade later.[1] Happy couples learn how to work around issues of disagreement and find a way to move on.

That is certainly how it works in my house. I remember that when our children were still of elementary school age, we sent them away to summer camp for a month. I should pause here to tell you that I too went to summer camp, and it was not a good experience for me. I was homesick almost every day. But I stuck it out and still hold to that as a point of pride to this day. So when my kids went to summer camp and we got the daily fax from them describing how homesick they were, I was only mildly perturbed. Then, when they upped the ante, telling my wife, Susan, and me how they were starving to death, enduring neglectful camp counselors, and feeling devoid of any friendships, I knew that they were playing hardball. But I wasn't going to cave; to me, this was a rite of passage, and I knew my kids would survive as I had.

My wife felt differently. She was sure there was something drastically wrong with the camp and that our children needed to be saved. So, two weeks into their camp adventure, Susan and I drove up to rural New Hampshire to "rescue" our children. I thought it was the wrong thing to do.

Whenever this issue comes up in our house, the intensity of emotion I felt comes back to me in waves. I still think Susan denied our children an educational and life-changing experience. And the intensity of emotion that Susan felt comes back to her equally as strongly. In fact, I'm sure that when Susan reads this passage in the book, she'll again remind me of how wrong I was, how blind I was, how heartless. It's as if we relive the event every time it's mentioned, and neither of us has conceded an inch in all these years. Arguments over how to raise the children are indeed emotional ones—especially for women. The Framingham Offspring Study in 2007 found that women rank children as the top reason for household arguments.[2]

So how do Susan and I handle this very delicate subject? We don't. This is an area that we have learned not to talk about. If we do talk about it, we do so briefly, and try to find ways to lower the intensity of the moment—such as by admitting that the other wins when it comes to being more stubborn—but we'll never admit that the other wins when it comes to who was right about that family event. We've learned that we'll never agree on this one, so we try not to bring it up (except when I write books!).

Do you have life events, beliefs, or hurts that can't be resolved? Join the club. In many cases, seeking to solve problems can be an exercise in futility, and you honor each other by agreeing to disagree.

Remember, in some cases you can either strive to be right or strive to stay together. Which will it be?

Your Partner Is Your Teacher

While I was home from college one summer, my friend Debbie sent me a letter with a postage stamp imprinted with the words "Learning Never Ends." She drew an arrow to the stamp adding "Bummer!" The idea that we'd be in school forever was indeed a drag. These days, of course, we look at our own children going to college and are quite envious of their opportunity. But I digress.

Now when I think of the stamp, I realize that it's true: we never do stop learning. And I realize that one of the most underrated institutions of higher learning is a place called home. Think about it. Since you created this group called family, haven't you learned new things? Perhaps you've discovered new ways of cooking? New ideas about politics? New card games? The appeal of unfamiliar music? Or the enjoyment of new friends or new places?

No doubt your partner has been an able teacher. But you still have a lot to learn—and you can learn it with greater success if you pay attention to the things you argue about. Conflict offers amazing clarity into the heart of a relationship to those who take the time to look and learn.

SECRETS FROM RESEARCH
Gay and Lesbian Couples in Conflict

John Gottman (of "Love Lab" fame) has determined that there are some important differences in the ways that gay and lesbian couples settle their differences compared to straight couples:[3]

Gay and lesbian couples are more upbeat in the face of conflict. They use more affection and humor when stressed.

Gay and lesbian couples use fewer controlling, hostile emotions in interactions. They are less inclined to use domination or fear—and more likely to use collaboration—in their interaction.

Gay and lesbian couples take fights less personally. Unlike the need for a 5:1 ratio of positive to negative interactions recommended for straight couples, gay couples appear less put out by negative comments and more likely to magnify positive interactions. When a negative comment crosses their partner's lips, they don't tend to take it as personally.

Gay and lesbian couples tend to show low levels of physiological arousal. When they get upset, they are better able to soothe each other, unlike straight couples, who get revved up when they are unhappy.

You probably have learned that if you push certain buttons, you can fire up a good argument. And no doubt your partner has learned to do the same. This knowledge shouldn't be kept stored away just for those angry occasions when you need a real zinger (*And your mother too!*). It's the kind of information you can use to better understand a person's heart and soul—your loved one's vulnerabilities and sensitivities.

Because conflict is inevitable, we all may as well take whatever benefit from it that we can. If you use conflict as an opportunity to better understand what makes your partner tick, then you can appreciate that learning isn't such a bummer after all—it's simply a form of enlightenment.

So as we move on in this chapter to explore some strategies for dealing with conflict, stay open to the fact that even when your partner infuriates you, he or she may be offering you an opportunity to learn, grow, and solidify the strength of your family—if you remember to watch, listen, and learn.

FAIR FIGHT FACT 2: WE ALL NEED TO BE HEARD

Imagine you came home one day, full of excitement because you found out that your poetry submission was just accepted for publication in the *New Yorker*. Unable to wait even a moment longer, you spill out the good news as you rush in the door. You look eagerly into the eyes of your partner, then your kids, then your cat, waiting to see what they think of this amazing accomplishment.

Then your beloved mate stares blankly at you, blinks a couple times, and responds, "Do you think we should plant more roses or switch to tomatoes this year?" Your adorable child says, "When are we gonna eat?" Your cat just stares at you.

How do you think you would feel? Most of us would have the same annoyed reaction: "I just told you what might be the single most important thing that has happened to me this year, and you all act as if I didn't say a thing. You didn't even acknowledge what I said! I feel as if I'm not even here! How can I ever get through to you?"

Yes, it feels pretty rotten to go unheard. In fact, in case you didn't catch the importance of the title of this section, I'll rephrase: *the most important need of a person is to be heard.*

Stuck Waiting for a Response

Here's why making someone feel heard is so important: when someone makes an effort to communicate with you, it's as if that person's brain goes into a holding pattern waiting for a response.

The conversation, the flow of intended emotion, and the interaction can't move forward while that person's brain is holding its mental breath. Yes, I know that brains don't really breathe, but if they did, just imagine the brain of a speaker getting bluer and bluer, waiting for the signal to breathe again. And that signal, pure and simple, is confirmation that someone heard what was said.

If you *do* make that person feel heard, whether with a nod, a grunt, an uh-huh, or certainly a more appropriate "That's so wonderful, honey!" then again, with a whoosh, the air rushes out of the mental lungs, and all goes back in order. Moreover, the brain is now able to receive incoming information.

If you *do not* act in a way that makes someone feel heard, the opposite happens. The brain can't move forward. It waits and waits and waits for some sign of confirmation and affirmation. While waiting, the speaker may choose to repeat the point, to shut down and give up, or to lash out with resentment or anger. Being unheard will *not* allow the brain to be open to what *you* have to say. So don't even think about sharing news of *your* day or foolishly asking what's for dinner.

Kids Need to Be Heard Too

This negative reaction to feeling unheard is especially evident in children. Early in childhood development, a child's sense of self is very dependent on the mirroring he gets back from his parents. Picture the eight-year-old boy riding down the street on his bike, hands high in the air, saying "Look ma, no hands!" By showing approval or shock or irritation, you are serving a critical role in your child's development by making him feel heard.

Likewise when your daughter comes home, eager to show you her A+ in algebra, she needs a sign of recognition. By acknowledging your children's communication with you, you assure them that they matter and are not invisible. Remarkably, they become more open to hearing what you have to say.

If you don't give this acknowledgment, kids learn to assume that you're not interested. Soon they stop talking. After that they stop listening. Then the field is set for battle. When you sit down to tell your teenager that you're not pleased with the friends she is hanging out with, and she gets up and says, "Whatever," she may feel on some level that she's just letting you know what it feels like to go unheard—terrible.

How Men and Women Listen Differently

When I treat heterosexual couples, one of the most common complaints voiced by women, hands down above all others is "He doesn't listen." So, is it true that men really have a listening problem?

Not really, but research does show that women and men listen differently. Because the speech and auditory centers of the brain are more developed in women than in men, when women listen, they tend to use more verbal acknowledgment and nod their head more, in order to encourage more verbal communication. Also, as we saw in Secret 2, women may be better able to use both hemispheres of their brains—the emotionally focused right side of the brain and the verbal-oriented left brain—in synchrony, so that processing emotions and details together is easier for them.

In contrast, men listen in a way that quite often makes women feel unheard. Their listening mechanisms are not wired into their emotional centers in the same way as women, so although they may offer verbal "I hear yous," their actions sometimes suggest something different.

Listening 101

Ready to listen? Here are some tried-and-true communication basics. If you consistently follow these three rules when communicating with family members, you'll soon see that they give you a powerful and direct way to crank up the level of happiness in your family.

1. Remove Distractions

If someone in your family wants to tell you something, it will be tough for you to make that person feel heard if you're working the thread through a sewing machine needle or moving on to the next level in Halo. The simple act of turning away from a distraction and giving your direct attention to the other person sends a powerful message of respect and love. If you're watching TV, turn it off (don't just put it to mute); if you're on the computer, shut down the screen; if you're reading a recipe for tonight's meal, put down the recipe card and look up.

Single mom Ella, for example, is a client of mine who runs her architectural business from home. She told me that whenever she sat at her drafting table, it was as if it activated a "Mommy! Mommy!" switch in her two school-age children. She needed to get her work done, but was thwarted by her kids' desire for her attention. What we determined was that all day long, Ella was giving her children *half* the attention they needed. When she wasn't working, she was so busy doing tasks around the house that she didn't have a chance to connect with the children. Because she felt guilty about not spending time with the children during the nonwork day, she didn't want to shut them out completely when she was at work, so she would allow them to talk to her from time to time, but, again, she wasn't able to give them their full attention.

"Giving someone half your attention is as bad as giving none of your attention," I told her, and we worked out a plan.

Now, when the children come home from school, Ella stops doing chores and sits with the children, allowing them to talk. She practices other good listening techniques (that we will discuss here) and makes sure that her children get a chance to discuss all the events of the day. She then asks the children to help with some of the chores (such as putting clothes away or sweeping the front stoop); afterward she stops again to thank them and acknowledge their efforts. When Ella sets time to go to work, she tells the children that this is time that she cannot listen to them, but gives them ideas on how to structure their time.

"My oldest one likes to write," she says, "so I give her a little journal to keep. When I'm done working, she and I sit for a few minutes and review the journal." Ella stops to take time to listen, and in the end, she gets more time to accomplish things, not less.

We all must make time every day to give each of our family members our *undivided* attention.

2. Clarify

Michael and Tiffany saw me in my office because their unusual lifestyle was starting to cause some problems in their relationship. Tiffany worked in a hospital during the day, but Michael was the main breadwinner, running several night clubs and constantly sponsoring media events. As Tiffany began to describe some of her concerns, Mike's cell phone went off. No, not a call, but a text, and Michael proceeded to text back while Tiffany spoke to me about problems in the relationship. Before we preceded, I referred Michael back to my first point: remove distractions. With his cell phone now turned off, we were ready to proceed to rule 2: clarify.

ME: (*addressing Michael*) When Tiffany is home and you're at work, she's worried about the people you might be spending time with. While you may see it as just being "friendly," she may be thinking that there's more going on than just getting a good photo op. She's worried that despite your good intentions, the women who are in the pictures may be making moves on you.

MICHAEL: Well, Doc, she's got to see that I have a job to do. (*Notice that Michael responded to me, but I'm not sure that he understood me. If I don't first make sure I feel understood, then everything he will say from this moment forward will fall on deaf ears—mine and his wife's.*)

ME: Hold on a minute, Michael. Before you begin to explain your job, I want to make sure that you understand what it is that Tiffany might be feeling. Could you take a moment to repeat back what I said, so that I can be sure you understood?

MIKE: I heard what you said!

ME: Okay, Mike, great, but do me a favor and repeat it back to me so that I can be sure that you heard it the way that I meant it.

MIKE: Yeah. No problem. You said that . . . I think . . . something about me taking pictures with other women . . . like, that it was, like, I was making the move on them . . . Wait. No. Could you repeat it back to me again?

This dialogue between Michael and me is actually quite typical. Because Mike was so eager to try to get his point across, he heard only part of what bothered Tiffany, and he launched right into a defensive response.

When caught in an argument that's going around in circles, you too should make sure that you and your family members repeat back what is being said. This is a great way to clarify that the message sent out is the same one that is received. (It also cuts down on the ever-popular circular accusation of "I never said that!" "Yes you did!")

So our dialogue continued:

ME: What I think Tiffany's been trying to say is that she's worried about the women you hang out with at the club and wishes you'd recognize that some of the women that you think are just friends may be on the make for you. Is that right, Tiffany?

TIFFANY: (nods her head)

MIKE: So, Tiffany, you think that the women that I'm in the pictures with may be on the make? For me? Even though I may not realize it?

TIFFANY: Yes! That's exactly what I've been worried about! Remember the time that you had that picture taken with Vanessa, and then the next day she called the house to talk with you? That seemed like more than just business to me.

3. Verify

Before Michael jumps in with an explanation, though, one very important step needs to take place. Michael must verify what Tiffany has said. By "verify" I don't mean that Michael must say, "Alas, dear Tiffany, you have uncovered my secret appeal to all women, and, indeed, they do want me passionately and incessantly." I mean, he must give her a sense that her feelings are valid to her. Something as simple as, "I can see why seeing me pose with beautiful women makes you feel threatened," says to Tiffany that she's not nuts. This seems pretty obvious, but many people try to counter another person's point of view with "You shouldn't feel that way."

That approach never works. People want to have their feelings acknowledged, even if the reasons underlying those feelings can't be substantiated.

This effort to make a person feel heard will reduce conflict among all your family members every time you remember to use it. Imagine that your daughter comes bursting through the door, exclaiming, "It's not fair! Tanya broke my lacrosse stick." It may be natural for you to counter with "I'm sure she didn't mean to break it." But first, it's important to hear your daughter out. Before offering your point of view or solution ("We'll sue that little guttersnipe, and her whole family too!"), clarify and verify: "Oh dear. Too bad. That was a great stick; you scored so many goals with it. It stinks to have someone break your stick." Then, once you've verified those feelings, you can find out exactly what happened.

The following three basic Fair Fight Facts each help you and your family members resolve your conflicts, but the key to applying each one successfully rests on your ability to first listen, clarify, and verify. Then you can respond in a way that strengthens your family ties.

FAIR FIGHT FACT 3:
WE NEED TO TREAT EACH OTHER WITH RESPECT TO SURVIVE CONFLICT

The Happy Family Survey that produced much of the core material for this book asked participants to choose from among given values the top few that bound them together as a family. (See Secret 1 for the values included on that list.) If a person felt that an important value was missing, he or she could write in that value.

Of all the write-in suggestions, respect was mentioned most often. It's obvious that the role of respect in the family definitely deserves mention and attention.

Let's take a good look at what respect means and how such a simple idea weaves its way in and out of family dynamics. As you were growing up, the concept of respect was probably a part of your education. As children, many of us were cautioned that we must at all times "respect our elders." In our evolving brains, we came to understand that that meant something like: "Don't talk back to someone who's older than you, even if you think he is wrong." And remember those high school assemblies where guest lecturers came and tried to teach you (and the guy who was shooting spit balls at the back of your neck) about how to get along with your peers? Yup, sure enough, it was the R-word all over again.

Perhaps we don't use the same direct, unquestioning approach nowadays, preferring to allow children themselves to determine who warrants their respect (although in many communities in America and the world, elders are still considered worthy of veneration), but in these times of affirmative action lawsuits, sensitivity trainings, and diversity mandates that demand zero tolerance for playground harassment, bullying, verbal abuse, and physical abuse, the message of respect is still drilled into the heads of our children.

By now we all get the message: all humans should be treated as if their beliefs and feelings matter. If that message is understood and practiced in your family, you will find that you'll survive the myriad disagreements that are part of being a family. You fight, you disagree, you argue, you fume—but you always respect the other person. You survive as a family.

What Respect Looks Like

If I asked you what kind of respect would help your family members survive disagreement, you might find it hard to say exactly. Respect fits in that category called "I know it when I see it." It's pretty obvious that when the pope walks into the room and a cardinal bows and kisses his ring, that's respect! When a teen gives up his seat on the crowded bus to an elderly person, that's respect. And when a mother-in-law bites her tongue rather than criticize her daughter-in-law's child-rearing methods, that's respect.

We also know what disrespect looks like. It's the open palm of a teenager staring you in the face, saying "Don't talk to me." It's in our daily lives when someone flips us the bird and tells us to blow it out our behinds. Yep, that's disrespect at its finest.

And when it comes to the family, disrespect again comes in many forms. You may feel the sting of disrespect when you have an opinion that someone in your family doesn't pay attention to. Or it may show itself when you speak up and your mate ridicules your idea. Perhaps you've seen the ugly side of disrespect when your kids go into a tantrum and say you're the dumbest human being ever to walk the face of the earth.

Earning Respect

It's only natural that as individuals spend more time together, they will find things that irritate, annoy, or otherwise rub them the wrong way. That's when the desire to act respectfully gets put to the test. Take this case as an example. One woman I see in my office had only recently recovered from a nearly deadly bout of pneumonia, so she promised her husband that she'd never smoke again. About a month after leaving the hospital, however, she began to go out during work breaks to sneak a puff or two on a cigarette with her friends. When her husband found out, he went ballistic! Did she still deserve respect after putting her life and the welfare of the family at risk again? It's easy to see how he felt betrayed and how she probably felt belittled by his angry reaction.

Children, likewise, should be granted respect, but when a seventeen-year-old forgets to put gas in the family car, leaves the car stranded on the roadside when it inevitably runs dry, and then takes off in a friend's car to enjoy the rest of the night out, how are we able to demonstrate respect to this teen? When these conflicts arise, they threaten the foundation of a family—unless the underlying layer of respect can withstand the hit. And respect does not mean blanket acceptance of intolerable behavior. Respect doesn't mean you have to like all aspects of any family member's behavior. But respect does mean that you always treat all family members with dignity and seek a way to understand the world through their eyes.

So how should the husband of the woman who continued to smoke after her pneumonia express his anger and disappointment while still respecting his wife? How can parents let their teen know that irresponsible use of the family car is unacceptable, without showing disrespect for him as a human being? It's not easy when the first thought that comes to mind sounds something like *How can you be so stupid!* But if the members of these families want to survive the argument and keep the core of the family strong, they'll take a deep breath and remember to avoid the hostile responses found in the next Fair Fight Fact.

FAIR FIGHT FACT 4: A HOSTILE START RESULTS IN A HARSH END

As you begin to read this section, please remember that the message of this chapter is not "Happy families never fight." It's a given that you *will* fight with your partner, your kids, your siblings, your in-laws, and yes, even with the family pet. It's the *way* you fight that determines whether the predominant mood in your household is one of anger, disappointment, resentment, and unhappiness, or one of peace, acceptance, trust, and happiness. You actually can control the family attitude—*if* you can reduce the level of hostility that fuels your arguments.

Ha! you say. Arguments are all about hostility. What's the point of arguing if I have to be polite about it?

When you put it that way, fair fighting starts to sound like one of those how-to book suggestions that sounds good in theory, but never works in real life. But I know that nonhostile fighting can work because I myself and so many of my clients have used it with great success. The premise is really quite doable and practical.

Remember These Four Words

When couples come to see me, before they leave the office I usually give them a list of four words, and I warn them that at their next visit there will be a pop quiz, so it's important to memorize all four of them.

Before I began to study relationships, I might have guessed that the four words might be, "Yes dear, you're right," or "Honey, I love you." Saying those phrases wouldn't hurt, but they're not the words I ask couples to commit to memory. The four powerful words that can change the way the members of your family fight and recover from those fights are all negative words—words that label four behaviors that researchers say can predict a failed relationship. These powerful words are

1. Criticism

2. Defensiveness

3. Stonewalling

4. Contempt

Researcher John Gottman, who has studied the destructive impact of these elements within a relationship, called them the "Four Horsemen of the Apocalypse" because of the catastrophic effects that these behaviors can wreak.[4] The presence of these behaviors can destroy any family—nuclear, blended, step- or foster, extended, gay or lesbian, single-parent. They can be lethal.

The good news is that these negative weapons are identifiable and avoidable. By decreasing their use and increasing healthier actions, you can turn the quality of your communication around to make your point, clarify your feelings, and propose changes without showing disrespect.

Let's look at these behaviors one at a time.

Criticism

Nobody's perfect. Okay, that's a given. But still, if you can't criticize, how can you let others know what's bothering you and what they need to change in order to stop bothering you? Criticizing or putting the offending person in his or her place and assigning blame are commonly used strategies in any family conflict. That's why it is quite likely that the husband of the nicotine addict or the parents of the irresponsible teen must avoid slipping into a shouting match that includes a lot of finger wagging and name calling.

We have all tried this method of showing the offending family member the error of his or her ways, but what comes naturally is not always most effective. Human psychology shows us that most people do not change their negative ways when shouted at or otherwise abused by violent opposition. Instead, they feel angry, disrespected, defensive, and powerless to change their behaviors in the future. Still, you sure have a right to lodge a complaint—just don't wrap it in criticism.

Criticisms and complaints are not at all the same thing. Criticisms attack the offender; complaints attack the offender's actions. Big difference. Let's say that your son Chris returns home around midnight after his fun night out and casually mentions that the family car is across town and that he needs a ride to a gas station and then back to his car. A critical approach to this situation would be: "Are you *nuts*?! How can forget to put gas in the family car and then abandon it? You'll be the death of me yet!"

Now, as a father, I can tell you that when my kids do something irresponsible like this, I actually have to wonder if in fact they might *be* stupid (although psychological testing has refuted that assertion). But calling an irresponsible teen "stupid" shows disrespect, and being critical of his actions does nothing to solve the problem. Just the opposite, because it usually drags down the quality of the relationship. The criticism ends up being a reflection of how intolerant—and fed up— the criticizer is, not a fair assessment of the person being blamed.

But having said that, I absolutely don't mean that you have to let your family members walk all over you (or lose the family car!). You have the right and the responsibility to lodge a complaint and then you can offer to work with the offending party to right things. That's not criticism; it's information.

You might try this: "You know, Chris, it's your responsibility to maintain the car, and it's not right for you to expect me to bail you out of this mess in the middle of the night."

The husband of the nicotine addict might say, "We've always tried to stay healthy in our household, and it's hard for me to understand or accept that you may be smoking again, especially with all that happened to you."

Remember, complaining is not necessarily a negative thing—as long as it is not accompanied by its evil cousin—criticism.

Criticism busters. One way to steer clear of criticism when stating a complaint is the old trick of using "I" statements. This is an easy strategy that happy families use to avoid laying blame. Imagine being the director of a major Hollywood production. You have control of the camera. Now imagine you're producing the scene where Chris walks in at midnight without the car. Instead of putting the camera on Chris, you tell your cameraman to swing the camera to Chris's parent (in this case, you). What emotion do you see?

SECRETS FROM RESEARCH
The Family Complainer

So who is the biggest complainer in your family? If practice makes perfect, that would be the female. In most heterosexual households, women lodge more complaints than men.[5] Interestingly, among the gay couples who come to my practice for relationship issues, the "spouse" who is identified as the one having primary responsibility in the domestic arena tends to be the one who complains more.

Upset, shock, worry, annoyance? When you start with an "I" statement, it's a way of expressing your own feelings and attaching them to an event that prompts them. "Chris is an irresponsible slob" is a statement that puts the camera on Chris. Now try putting the camera on yourself.

First, voice your complaint composed earlier: "You know, Chris, it's not right for you to expect me to bail you out of this mess in the middle of the night."

Then tag on the "I" statement: "I feel upset that I have to be the one to pick up the pieces when you don't follow through on your responsibilities." With this simple but powerful change in focus, you avoid putting down your son and are able to work toward a resolution (which, in our house, would consist of having Chris call a friend to drive him around looking for a gas station and then back to the family car).

In the same way, the husband of the smoker can avoid the negative fallout from criticism but still get his wife to see his point of view by following his complaint with an "I" statement, such as "I'm worried that you'll get addicted to smoking again, and that you'll become sick and may not pull through it this time. I'm so afraid to lose you, honey."

A nonhostile complaint and an "I" statement can be used to address just about any problem in your family with any member of your family. Combine this approach to trouble with the following advice regarding defensiveness, and you've tamed two of the four wild horses of the Apocalypse.

Defensiveness

Those who don't yet understand the negative effect of criticism on a happy family life may continue to shoot off critical comments by playing the old blame game. "It's always your fault that we're late!" "Why do you have to be so picky?" "You don't even try to understand how I feel." Sound familiar? Statements like these probably are a part of many family conflicts.

When you are hit with the critical finger of blame, how do you react? Let's say, for example, that you arrive home late (again) because you had an important piece of business to finish that will add a nice chunk of change to your bank account. Before you can explain why you missed dinner again, your partner meets you at the door with "Once again, you didn't think of anyone but yourself."

What would you say? Many of us will run the defense: "That's not true." "This is my job." "It's not my fault!" Again . . . sound familiar?

Let's take a look at how avoiding a defensive response and, instead, substituting good listening skills can change the direction of an argument.

I was Luke's supervisor during his training to become a psychiatrist. At that time, he had been married to Adriana for almost ten years. Luke told me he was perplexed by her criticism of him. Rather than expressing joy at how hard he worked (which in the field of medicine is undeniably an excellent attribute), she was angered by what she perceived to be the unfair burden of child care and home care placed on her shoulders while he worked.

Luke and I would have long conversations about the strains of his work, and the effort it takes to keep relationships outside the office on track. But Luke had a wonderful attitude toward the situation, which ultimately led to a stronger relationship with his wife.

"When she offers up a complaint, my first instinct," Luke confessed, "is to explain to her how she's not seeing it right and how I am not the one to blame. But I've learned to keep that information to myself. Saying that would make Adriana feel like I was invalidating her emotions. If there's one thing being a psychiatrist has taught me, it's that emotions are real, and they can't easily be brushed aside."

Instead of fighting back with defensive criticism of his own, Luke took a different tack: he became a good listener who let his wife feel heard. "When she confronts me as I walk through the door with a sarcastic, 'Thanks for showing up and lending a hand around here,' I try not to counter with 'Well, thanks for appreciating all the long hours I put in so I can give you and the baby a better life!' Instead, I ask her what her day has been like; I let her know that I want to hear more about why she feels drained. Then I verify what I heard, and reflect it back. I agree with her that she has those feelings for a reason, and then I ask what I can do to help."

Luke told me that on some days, she said, "I'm glad you asked!" and gave him a honey-do list. But other days, she didn't really need anything tangible at all and expressed thanks to him for listening. A potential clash easily averted.

Luke had learned that fighting from a defensive position is a no-win strategy. So to nurture peace in his family life, he responded to criticism by saying, "Tell me why you think that might be the case, and help me figure out what I can do to solve this problem." I have no doubt that ever since we had those talks, Luke's family is a happy one.

Stonewalling

Everyone in your family has a unique style of fighting. One person may get sarcastic; another may get loud; one may even tend to break things. But usually there is also the person who chooses to stonewall.

When a person stonewalls, he shuts down from conversation or conflict, or simply walks away. This approach may seem peaceful and inoffensive because, really, the silent person doesn't say or do anything that obviously hurts the relationship. But here's the problem: that person doesn't say or do anything to help the relationship either. And he may know, secretly or with passive aggression, that walking away can drive his wife nuts. So remember that sometimes stonewalling can be a ploy to win a fight and annoy the heck out of an opponent.

Studies show that whereas women speak up and lodge complaints over 80 percent of the time, men are the ones to shut down 85 percent of the time.[6] It's my belief that one of the reasons that men tend to stonewall is that they aren't comfortable with the feelings generated when they are upset. In the board room and on the football field, men can assert dominance and vent their rage. At home, men in America often feel that they're getting the message that "if you raise your voice, I'll feel threatened and may accuse you of abusing me." It's not just that. Most men don't really want to fight. They don't want to see their wives in the one-down position.

"Nobody wins that way," they reason, "so I'd better stay away."

Females stonewall too (it's known as the silent treatment), but not as often as men. This is a good thing, because the silent treatment not only corrodes the atmosphere of the home but also appears to be terribly hard on the woman's health. A long-term study of residents of Framingham, Massachusetts, showed that it really didn't matter all that much what brought a couple to the boiling point; if a woman had strong emotions and didn't speak her mind, she was four times as likely to die during the study period as women who shared their feeling with their husbands.[7]

Many women have told me that they will use stonewalling to avoid angry confrontations and to keep their lethal criticisms in check, but these efforts to keep the peace are not effective in the long term. Assuming that the woman doesn't die of repressed anger, she will still carry around that unspoken resentment and unhappiness. That's no way to nurture a happy family in the long run. The unspoken complaints turn into resentment and are bound to pop up again and again because they are left unresolved in the silence.

Contempt

Criticism is sure to squash happiness in any family. But contempt can kill it forever.

Contempt is motivated by a wish to hurt someone emotionally or to demonstrate outward disgust. You can always recognize contempt by its telltale signs of rolling eyes and sneering lips. Contempt is mean, ugly, and a sign of major trouble.

In fact, unlike the occasional critical comment that pops up now and then in any family, contempt doesn't show its ugly face until criticizing becomes entrenched as a way of daily communication, and respect becomes a foreign country. Often people in this stage are so filled with hostility, anger, disrespect, and resentment that they can't seem to shut off the contempt valve. That's why it's hard to rid contempt from your family dynamics once it has sunk its teeth in.

There is a solution, but it takes a bit of mental gymnastics. In order to sweep contempt out of your life, you must replace it with positive thoughts, and focus on positive attributes. If she shows up late from work, you must replace the "She doesn't have any idea of how much I suffer when she's not here to have dinner with me," with "She's working hard to do her part to make a contribution." If he just paid $200 for a new set of golf clubs (assuming you're not in Chapter 11 bankruptcy), you must shift from "He's so inconsiderate" to "He really seems to enjoy taking care of himself; I hope that he enjoys this." I told you it wouldn't be easy, but it's worth the mental effort.

I met a woman at a book signing who began to describe her frustration with her husband who, she took pains to point out to me, was four years her senior. She's the main breadwinner in the home, and she's also the one in charge of the bills. So she was particularly annoyed when he took the car in for service while she was away for the weekend. "He didn't realize that I had a coupon for 10 percent off. The job cost $1,500, so that was a savings of $150 he prevented us from getting." I could hear her leaning toward criticism ("He always does things like this!") and contempt ("I'll never be able to change him; it's like he doesn't think!"), but then I noticed a shift in her facial expression. "Well, he really doesn't buy anything for himself, so I guess I have to look at that $150 that we could have saved as a treat that he bought for himself." The facts didn't change, but because she was able to shift the way she looked at it, she let go of her resentment and was ready to forge ahead in this marriage of thirty-plus years.

If having a happy family is important to you, and you've no plans to bust it up, then it's vital that when you talk to yourself (and we all do!), you replace those negative comments with positive, affirming thoughts. That's how you keep contempt from robbing you of the happiness you desire.

FAIR FIGHT FACT 5: THE FIGHT MUST BE OVER BY BEDTIME

Remember that old adage "Don't go to bed angry"? Turns out there's scientific proof that this is wise advice. Studies show that couples who learn to make up, either through reapproaching each other in a loving way or by apologizing or by helping the other person feel better, are likely to have a long-lasting relationship; couples who cannot are likely to split up. That's sobering, isn't it?

It's true that anger can make it almost impossible for all family members to solve their problems with each other. That's because there's a part of the brain that lights up when feelings are riled up. It's called the amygdala. The amygdala serves a very important role in your life because it lets you know when there's trouble ahead.

Studies of monkeys show that they hate snakes, and when they see them, they panic! But when researchers removed the amygdala from the brains of some of the monkeys, the snakes didn't bother them at all. Of course it wouldn't be ethical to do such research in humans (and some people feel the same about the monkeys), but if this same experiment were performed on humans, there would be a whole lot of us walking around with snake bites—we would lose our ability to respond quickly and emotionally.

One of the reasons the amygdala is such a good thing to have is that it shuts down the "thinking" part of your brain (the frontal lobes) and allows fight-or-flight instincts to take over. When a potentially frightening event happens, such as taking a turn on a highway and seeing a bunch of cars involved in a multivehicle collision in front of you, you don't want to say to yourself, "Gee, I wonder what the formula is to determine the rate of deceleration with a beginning speed of 85 mph, and what the coefficient of friction would be on a pair of Goodyear tires?" No, you want to be able to react immediately by putting your foot on the brake, adjusting your steering, and getting out of the way of that oncoming truck as soon as possible.

This is similar to what happens at home when you get upset. Let's say you return from food shopping and your mate offers to help you put the groceries away. As you're mindlessly chatting about the price of cereal these days, you see him put the bananas in the refrigerator. "Please don't do that," you ask. "You always do that, and the bananas never ripen as they should."

"Are you saying," he replies, "that every time I've put the bananas in the refrigerator, I've ruined them? That's ridiculous. My mother always put the bananas in the refrigerator."

"Well," you say calmly as anger rises through your entire body and blood rushes to your amygdala, "there are lots of things your mother does that are just plain wrong."

"What? Now you have a problem with my mother?"

You can see where this argument is going. Yeah, I know it's not the same as nearly getting in a car crash, but, funny thing is, when your alarm system gets triggered, it really doesn't matter whether it's over a pileup on I-95 or the great banana debate. When the amygdala switch gets turned on, it takes some time for the blood flow to shift back to the reasoning part of the brain; sometimes it will take up to half an hour before you can make good decisions again (and why the issue of where to keep bananas is not going to be solved rationally during this conversation).

That's where patching things up after an argument comes in. When you're with your loved ones and your amygdala switches on, your loving feelings toward them turn off. That's not the time to turn off the light and roll over and go to bed in a state of unresolved warfare. Give yourself time to cool down. Then you can make this important decision: What's more important—fighting to be right or fighting to keep your family together? I have to agree with that wise old adage that insists on your making up before falling asleep.

THE FAIR FIGHT

Talking about how to fight fair reminds me of the karate classes I took when I was in medical school. My instructor demonstrated a principle that, despite years of medical and scientific study, would never have occurred to me. She explained that when an opponent comes at you with a roundhouse kick (you know, the kind of kick in the movies where the hero, on the brink of exhaustion, swings fully around in a circle and delivers a kick to the face of his foe), the best strategy is not to try to get away. When your opponent begins to twirl, you should move *toward* the body of the person throwing the kick, thus causing the kick to lose its power and reducing the risk of serious injury.

Applied to household fights, the same principle holds. When you feel the need to run from conflict or to remain rigid and defensive and try to take the kick, it may actually be better to move in closer. Taking a step toward your family member to listen, clarify, and verify will decrease the impact of the blow and help you work toward solving the problem. Moving in, rather than away, will also ensure that you limit your use of criticism, defensiveness, stone-walling, and contempt—all products of unresolved anger.

Being able to move toward those you love for better under-standing—even when you're embroiled in an argument—allows you to put negative feelings behind you and imagine a brighter future. This is one of the skills of people who can bounce back when knocked down by life and get back to working on building a happy family. We'll talk more in the next chapter about how they do that.

Happy Families . . . Bounce

Some say, sure, it's easy to be a happy family when life is good. When money isn't a problem, when the kids are little angels, when we're all healthy, when the in-laws are loving and supportive, when partners are joyfully in love—boy, are we happy! But what about real people in real families with some real trouble? Can we be expected to be happy when times are tough?

Yes.

Bad things happen. Financial hardship, hospitalization, relocation, problems at school, even physical abuse—they happen all the time in all families. Some families fall apart under the strain; others take the hit, but bounce right back. Why is that? Why can some families, but not others, weather the tough times and remain strong, loving, and happy? The key secret of the families who are able to bounce is found in one word: *resiliency*.

VOTING FOR RESILIENCY

Resiliency is a common term, usually associated with toughness or durability; for example, the balsam fir is a *resilient* tree, able to withstand harsh northern winters. In human psychology terms, it often refers to the capacity of an individual to recover quickly from a misfortune or trauma and maintain an established pattern of functioning. More simply, resiliency is the quality of families that can stretch and bounce back when confronted with challenges! Not only is this ability important, but, according to the individuals who completed the Happy Family Survey, it is the single most important factor in keeping a family together.

When asked what contributed most to a happy family, respondents were asked to rank the following six factors: (1) agreeing about money, (2) resiliency, (3) doing a lot of activities as a family, (4) having children grow up with both biological parents, (5) living within an hour's distance from the children's grandparents, and (6) attending religious services weekly.

Resiliency was given the number one vote more than any other factor. When I analyzed the data, I found an interesting phenomenon. This choice of resiliency as an important factor in a happy family didn't waver according to the type of family; whether respondents were in a traditional nuclear, step, blended, single-parent, or gay or lesbian family, all recognized that if you have resiliency, then you have the necessary ingredient to have a happy family.

Secrets of Happy Families

When Older Kids Can Pitch In

With baby #4, I was in the hospital for a month; my older kids had to pitch in without Mom around, and my husband had to be both Mom and Dad for a month. The kids only saw me once a week. It was hard, but we made it through; the kids were strong and happy after it, and we all still remember seven years later.

—Felicia, 38, married 13 years

Unfortunately, having a family that can weather the slings and arrows of life's outrageous fortune doesn't come easy. That's why its integral role in family dynamics is too often kept a secret.

GOT RESILIENCY?

If resiliency is what's needed to cement the bonds of a happy family, then where can you get it? It would be oh-so-nice if we could simply flip through a catalogue and order it from the Resiliency Store or, better still, go to eResiliency.com, download it, and save the cost of shipping. But, as you know, resiliency isn't acquired through usual commercial means; it begins in the chromosomes of the developing child and builds within a human being through the influence of the environment.

Resilient Genes

You're not just handed an "I've got resiliency" card at birth, but your genes do play a role. Twin studies show that how people respond to negative events can be inherited. When researchers looked at the chances of a person developing posttraumatic stress disorder (PTSD—a psychiatric condition of anxiety symptoms, avoidant behavior, and distressing recollections of traumatic events), they found that of all the variables that could cause the syndrome, genetics account for one-third of the equation.

Other studies show that differences in inheritance explain why children with different genetic makeups show different degrees of alarm when bad things happen to them.[1] In fact, scientists have studied abused children and found that one variation on the gene for serotonin (the brain chemical that antidepressants such as Prozac or Lexapro increase) can affect a child's vulnerability to maltreatment.[2] Researchers state that these types of genes "potentially serve as predictors of both risk and resilience for adult PTSD among survivors of child physical and sexual abuse."[3] So, remarkably, our ability to bounce back (or not) is in part an inherited trait.

SECRETS FROM RESEARCH
Gender Differences in Response

Much of a person's response to stress occurs without any conscious awareness, and often occurs differently for males and females. When men begin to feel pressure mount, they become more physically charged up, engaging the fight-or-flight response: they have a rise in blood pressure, heart rate, and skin temperature. They tend to clam up and withdraw socially, and put their sole focus on single-handedly managing the oncoming challenge. Women, in contrast, will often become more social and tender, and they reach out more for support from others when disaster is at hand. This "tend or befriend" phenomenon may explain why women want to talk when under pressure, and why their equally stressed male partners don't want to listen!

Resiliency-Building Experiences

Inherited levels of resiliency don't entirely explain the differences in the way people respond to trauma. Background experience has a strong role to play as well. A moderate amount of stress impinging on our lives can actually help make us mentally stronger and better prepared to handle new problems, and less overwhelmed with emotion when problems do come up. In order to maintain the mental balance we need to feel happy, it helps a lot to have been exposed to small amounts of stress, to build up our defenses—like an inoculation.

When researchers experimented with adolescents by exposing them to a one-time stressful situation in a laboratory setting, they found that if the teens had faced mild, controllable stress in childhood, by adolescence they handled tense situations with reduced blood pressure and heart rates. Clearly, the ability to stay cool under pressure develops more in those who have successfully weathered stressful childhood experiences, such as loss of friendships or a death in the family. In adulthood, these people appear to be more resistant to significant losses, such as the loss of a loved one or divorce.

In contrast, *major* childhood stress, such as abandonment or abuse, is not an effective way of building resiliency. In fact, early emotional trauma can lead to long-term brain and behavior changes. Fortunately, studies show that even if children are exposed to exceptional childhood adversity, they can still recover and grow up to become strong adults.

The Kauai Longitudinal Study looked at 698 children with birth complications, poverty, family discord, and parental mental illness, and followed their progress for forty years.[4] As the study predicted, there were school difficulties, mental health problems, and teenage pregnancy for most of the high-risk children, but one-third of the children escaped having a painful adolescence. The main difference in the children who did well was the presence of emotional support by family, friends, teachers, and adult mentors. These individuals were positive role models during the children's impressionable years, and they provided consistent nurture and support. It was as if exposure to these supportive influences protected children against falling apart in their teen years.

Moral of the story: it takes a village to raise a child.

Secrets of Happy Families

Family Support for Abused Daughter

My daughter had a relationship with an abusive male. It was ugly, and we went to court with a restraining order for her and myself (against him). She was pregnant with his child at the time, and now my daughter and granddaughter live with me, my husband, and my other two adult children, along with a disabled dog and various other critters. The baby will grow up without her biological father. The good thing is she will grow up surrounded by her Nana, Papa, and Aunt and Uncle who love her very much, and my daughter has all the help she needs.

—*Alicia, 44, married 27 years*

SOCIAL SUPPORT

Research has shown us the elements that correlate with resiliency. Top on this list is social support. There's no doubt that resilient people rely on others to help them through trying situations.

Many of us know from personal experience that having others by our side in times of trouble helps make us stronger. There are also medical studies supporting our observations; these studies demonstrate that social support enhances mental and physical health in many ways. We know, for example, that during a medical illness, low levels of social support are associated with depressive disorders, increased pain, suffering, and even death. In contrast, having a social network is associated with longer and happier lives. These are astonishing findings that clearly illustrate the power of surrounding ourselves with supportive, loving people.

Secrets of Happy Families

Family Support During Immigration

After immigrating to the United States from Romania, I don't think we could have made it if we weren't together as a family. We took turns supporting each other and the children during dire emotional and financial times. We supported each other in completing our educational and professional goals. We leaned on each other at times when things were not going well, and we celebrated (literally!) every accomplishment with our family and friends. We brought our parents to our new country, so our children can have the blessing of knowing their grandparents.

—*Margaret, 40, married 18 years*

The miracle of social support is thought to work through several modalities. It can

Help you measure the threat of a situation more realistically: "Oh, sweetheart, don't worry. That's just the way the pipes sound in old houses like this."

Help foster effective coping strategies: "Just ignore Uncle Ted when he starts to talk about his crazy ideological agenda!"

Increase feelings of self-esteem and abilities: "I know she'll go out with you; you're so charming."

Decrease rates of high-risk behavior: "Where do you think you're going with that knife balanced on your chin?"

Keep you on the straight and narrow of medical care: "Don't forget your checkup appointment on Monday."

Having a family to push, prod, cajole, encourage, and direct us through the winding maze of life directly contributes to our ability to face adversity and bounce back. Sure, many of us would like occasionally to come home to a quiet, empty house and enjoy the peace of solitude, but that momentary joy would soon be replaced by that empty feeling of loneliness, isolation, and even fear—fear that if something bad happens we'll have to face it alone. That's why happy families are the ones that accept the noise and occasional chaos in exchange for the support and love a family can give.

SECRETS FROM RESEARCH
Active Coping

According to Steve Southwick, one of my colleagues when I was at Yale University, "Most research has found that the active approach-oriented coping, and not the passive-avoidance strategies, are most effective in dealing with stressful situations."[5] Examples of these active coping styles include the following:

- Gathering information
- Acquiring resources, such as learning the skills, acquiring the tools, and gathering the knowledge
- Problem solving
- Decision making
- Seeking social support
- Being able to shift your way of seeing things when you get new information

In various studies, this active style of dealing with stress has been associated with fewer psychological symptoms and improved well-being. The take-home message here is that if we adopt a passive view of our life, focusing on blaming our problems on bad genes, bad parenting, bad circumstances, bad luck, or bad people, we'll actually start feeling . . . bad!

FACTORS OF RESILIENCY

Your family members are your teachers—they are there to show you how to bend, and not break, with the winds of adversity. Most often this happens unnoticed as you go from day to day, interacting with the people closest to you. Yet there are in fact certain identifiable family structures that teach these lessons and keep family members from snapping in that wind.

In order to see how resiliency works within the family structure, experts look at two aspects: *protective factors* that shape the family's ability to endure when confronted with stress, and *recovery factors* that promote the family's ability to bounce back from a crisis.

Protective Factors

Much in the same way that individuals have protective factors that shield them from the negative onslaughts of life (intact household, healthy diet, supportive network, and good genes, to name a few), families have features that will help them remain strong during times of adversity. Several of these features, such as conflict management, communication, leisure activities, routines, and family traditions and celebrations, are addressed throughout this book. They are the aspects of a family that, when consciously nurtured, can safeguard its members from the kinds of stress and trauma that bring down other, less well protected families.

Not all protective factors are equally as important over the life of the family. Researchers point to different life phases as requiring different stress reducers.[6] Across the top of Table 7.1, you'll see four stages of the life cycle: couple, childbearing/school age, teenage/young adult, and empty nest/retirement. For each of those stages, eleven critical adaptive qualities are needed to strengthen the family.

For instance, *financial management* is critical in the first three phases of the family, but less of an issue as the empty nest stage sets in. (Boy, do I know this feeling. I just say to myself, "Let me get my kids through college and then, maybe then, I'll have two nickels to rub together for myself!") *Health*, in contrast, is a critical concern as the members of a family age, but less of a worry in the relatively strong child-rearing years.

Looking at the life stage of your family, what are the factors most likely to guard against adversity? Across all stages, we see that celebrations, hardiness, time and routines, and traditions remain a

Table 7.1: Protective Factors Across Family Life Stages

Protective Factors	Couple	Childbearing/ School Age	Teenage/ Young Adult	Empty Nest/ Retirement
Accord: Balanced interrelationship among family members that allows them to resolve conflicts and reduce chronic strain.	✓	✓		
Celebrations: Acknowledging birthdays, religious occasions, and other special events.	✓	✓	✓	✓
Communication: Sharing beliefs and emotions with one another. Emphasis is on how family members exchange information and caring with each other.	✓	✓		✓
Financial Management: Sound decision-making skills or money management and satisfaction with economic status.	✓	✓	✓	
Hardiness: Family members' sense of control over their lives, commitment to the family, confidence that the family will survive no matter what.	✓	✓	✓	✓

Table 7.1: Protective Factors Across Family Life Stages, *continued*

Protective Factors	Couple	Childbearing/ School Age	Teenage/ Young Adult	Empty Nest/ Retirement
Health: The physical and psychological well-being of family members.	✓			✓
Leisure Activities: Similarities and differences of family member preferences for ways to spend free time.	✓			
Personality: Acceptance of a partner's traits, behaviors, general outlook, and dependability.	✓		✓	✓
Support Network: Positive aspects of relationships with in-laws, relatives, and friends.		✓	✓	
Time and Routines: Family meals, chores, togetherness, and other ordinary routines contributing to continuity and stability in family life.	✓	✓	✓	✓
Traditions: Honoring holidays and important family experiences carried across generations.	✓	✓	✓	✓

Source: Reprinted with permission from McCubbin and others, "Families Under Stress: What Makes Them Resilient," article based on the American Association of Family and Consumer Sciences Commemorative Lecture, Washington, D.C., June 22, 1997. www.cyfernet.org/research/resilient.html.

consistent need. The pattern here is obvious: no matter how old our family, we need to wear the armor of togetherness. We need to commit to our family and make sure that we celebrate who we are through the generations, acknowledge what we stand for in our traditions, and make sure that we spend time together by creating daily routines that allow us face-to-face time.

These are the protective factors that will guard us against stress and trauma. But no matter how well families are protected, they all will experience difficult times. That's why families also need the recovery factors to be in place.

Recovery Factors

Since the beginning of time, philosophers and religious leaders have pondered the mystery of why bad things happen to good people. I have my own ideas, which great thinkers may or may not agree with. But that's the point, isn't it? We each have to find our own way of explaining suffering.

Here's an insight from thirty-five-year-old Livvie, whom I "met" through the Happy Family Survey. She ranks herself and her family—now consisting of her husband and her dog—as extremely happy. Here's what she had to say:

> Well, from the dog's point of view, we, my husband, the dog, and I are a pack, and my husband is the leader. We, the dog and I, fall in line when something really important comes up. If my husband says there is a dangerous storm and for us to get in the basement, we move and ask questions later. It is his job to protect us, his family. It probably sounds old-fashioned, but it works for us. My husband treats me like a queen and I treat him like a king, and we've been doing that for 14 years.

Hats off to Livvie! But as I scrolled down further in the survey, where I asked for a description of the challenges her family faced, I read this:

We have weathered the loss of our precious daughter to heart disease and we've weathered job loss, homelessness (we camped out for five months once), and very tight money. Once we had nothing to eat for a week, but we're still kickin'! We got through the above by being optimistic and strong in character.

Wow! From Livvie's initial description of her "extremely happy" family where love and respect lay a strong foundation, I might have assumed that life had been kind to her and her husband. Boy, would I have been wrong. Yet her cloak of resiliency seems to have helped her recover from exceptionally difficult times and allowed her to bounce, rather than fall. Amazing.

None of us are immune from the hurts of being human. Of course we can, and should, work hard to build into our family structure the protective factors so important to strong families, but even they cannot always defend against all of life's surprises. Unexpected ill winds are an inescapable truth of life. I'm reminded of the old Yiddish saying, "Man plans, God laughs."

So when bad things do happen—and they will—we need to have a strong foundation built on the protective factors mentioned earlier in this chapter. Then we need the tools of recovery to bounce back.

These tools vary from one situation to the next, but the work of researchers with the Institute for Health and Disability at the University of Minnesota gives us some insights into recovery factors. These researchers looked at the stress experienced by families whose children suffered from severe disabilities.[7] They found that the following recovery factors contribute to positive outcomes:

- Families emphasize the positive and are not preoccupied with why the condition happened.

- Family members manage the demands of the child within the context of family life.

- Families have a coherent explanation of the cause of their child's condition that is consistent with their worldview.

I'm intrigued by this study because the strategies these families of children with disabilities used can also be applied effectively to other life situations. When the members of any family apply these recovery factors to the stress of family life, whether that be day-to-day common annoyances or the trauma of life-altering events, they are better able to survive and even benefit from the experience.

I saw these recovery factors at work in Livvie's responses to my survey. How could a person with so many reasons to be unhappy describe herself as "optimistic"? So I got in touch with Livvie and asked her to tell me more about her painful experience of losing her daughter to heart disease. With her permission, I share her words with you:

> Melsie was two-years-old when we found ourselves sitting in Dr. P.'s office. My daughter ran to the tall and skinny, and, because the pediatrician noticed some possible heart problem, we feared that it might be Marfan syndrome, a genetic disorder where the connective tissue doesn't function right. I wanted to hear that it wasn't Marfan, but as we sat across from the doctor he gently fed us the life-changing news: my little girl had Marfan syndrome.
>
> The doctor discussed the whys and hows of this, how the illness can stretch out the bones and make people taller, how the eye gets stretched, often resulting in a detached retina, and how lung disease and heart disease often cause problems later in life. I was just interested in all this information, because it was thought that Abraham Lincoln had Marfan, and, even though I am only five feet, I am blood related to Honest Abe.

After the diagnosis, Melsie saw the insides of a lot of doctors' offices. Insurance paid all of Melsie's bills so that made it possible for us to use what little else we had to give my two girls, Melsie and her big sister, Charmaine, ballet lessons, books, dolls, and trips to Sea World. Our family did all the things that most families do. We just did them with more challenges.

At one point Melsie had five or six doctors. There was the bone doctor and the eye doctor and the heart doctor and the physical therapists, and I ran myself ragged trying to keep up with it all. If one was to look at a picture of me during those years, it looks as if I am wearing eye makeup. Not so. I was exhausted but I refused to give in to it.

No, it wasn't always easy. Nor was it easy to deal with my oldest daughter. Charmaine was a smart little kid, and of course she saw all the attention that Melsie got, so I sat her down one day and asked her to look at her fingers. I asked her if she loved them. She said she did, and then I asked if one got slammed in the door, which one would she pay attention to. She said she'd pay attention to the one that hurt. Melsie was the one that got hurt.

People would ask me how I lived with that knowledge that at any day my daughter could die, and I told them I couldn't. Instead, we just lived. There were birthday cakes to be baked, chores to be done, schools to attend, boo-boos to be kissed, and doctors to be seen.

Melsie lived a lot longer than the doctor predicted. The years went by, and they saw me going to college. But when she was eighteen years old, Melsie had become weaker and had problems catching her breath, and once again we were in a doctor's office, Dr. M. this time. He was the top in his field of surgery, but he wasn't much on bedside manner. He wanted to keep Melsie and do surgery on her the next day. Motherhood instinct at the fore, I told him flat out no, and that I had a lot of questions, which he brushed off.

By the time we left the office I was building a head of steam. As I marched down a flight of stairs, Dr. M. asked us how we were. I told him I was pissed off because he wouldn't answer my questions. By the time I got to the bottom of the stairs I was yelling at the top of my lungs. I think that I'd had enough of doctors. I had enough of their "let's talk this way to stupid mothers." I yessed them for sixteen years, and by God they were not touching my flesh and blood until the questions were answered! Oh, I took the paint off the walls. I yelled all through the corridors on the way out to the parking lot and I yelled all the way to the car. I don't think I'd ever been in such a rage in all my life. I remember kneeling down beside the car, my face in the asphalt, my pent-up tears wetting the black pebbles.

Later that evening another doctor called me. He had an excellent bedside manner. He answered all my questions, and lovingly too. After two-and-a half-hours I was satisfied. Now at age eighteen, Melsie had the final say about surgery. I wanted to cry again for her. To have a decision like she faced at such a young age was just not fair. But, I had to remember that the concept of fairness was fine for a baseball game, but not much else. She assented to the surgery.

About three days later, as Melsie struggled with shortness of breath and general weakness, I put her in the car and we headed over the hill for the hospital. She signed the papers for surgery and I co-signed them. It was a done deal. This is what we thought was right.

I felt confident about it. After all, I saw her come through three back surgeries. I could easily wait for her to sail through heart surgery. In fact, I was so confident I went to a lecture on biochemistry while she was on the table. Dr. M. and I put our differences behind us, and I had every confidence in his skill as a surgeon.

But the operation didn't go well. Without going too far into the pathology of things, it wasn't long before trouble was brewing. Melsie's heart was sicker than anyone could have banked on, and believe me, she had all the pre-surgery tests. One of the assistant surgeons came out and asked my permission to do a bypass. I gave it. Dr. M. and his platoon of surgery people worked twenty-four hours on Melsie's heart. They installed an aortic balloon pump in the hope of giving her heart the rest it needed to beat on its own.

Finally they rolled her out of the operating theater and into the recovery room. I saw her about 1 AM, well into the next day. She was hooked up to enough machines to fly her to the moon, which she would have liked by the way. (She had just been accepted into UCSC's astrophysics program, and I was sure she was the next coming of Stephen Hawking.) Although her eyelids fluttered when I said her name, she was a very sick young woman. I knew she wasn't going to make it. Don't ask me how; mothers just know these kinds of things. She died in my arms later that day.

Melsie also knew she wasn't going to make it. She knew before I did. When high school girls get ready to go somewhere, they bring the full artillery. They have makeup, hairdryers, curlers, and an outfit for every contingency. It was a couple weeks after Melsie died that I realized that she brought nothing with her, save the little stuffed bunny who had seen every surgery since she was a third grader. She just got in the car and we drove off. She knew.

Now I want to know how did she get the courage and the guts and gumption to get silently in the car and go "gently into that good night"? I honestly don't know where stuff like that comes from. I remember leaving the hospital with the bunny, driving to a cliff over the ocean and screaming at the endlessly waving water. I wanted my baby back. I guess I thought the ocean could give her to me.

Melsie died on a Thursday and I was back in school the following Tuesday. Somehow I made it through the last of the exams and projects. I got through a lot of school by running the "Pomp and Circumstance" tune through my head. No lie. Some days it was the only thing that kept me going. Then the day came for the graduation wingding. When my name was called and I walked across the outdoor stage for my five seconds of glory, the entire staff of the college gave me a standing ovation. They didn't give it to anyone else, just me. I thought walking over to the podium, okay Melsie, while you're safe now, with no more pain and beyond care, this is, still and all, for you baby . . .

Livvie's story moved me deeply; in the face of tremendous challenges, she still kept her spirit afloat, and that's what makes her a resilient and even upbeat person today. If you too can remember to emphasize the positive, accept the things you can't change, and look for the big picture, it is likely that your family will not only recover from difficult times but also be able to put aside the setback, press on, and grow. Then surely you will all once again find family happiness.

DAILY RESILIENCY

Each of us has daily opportunities to help our family members learn how to bounce when they've had a bad day (or month, or year). Some of these opportunities are disguised as routine family activities, but they promote the growth of resiliency nevertheless. For example, resiliency can be taught by

Emphasizing cause and effect in life: "We sit down to a home-cooked meal because if we eat good foods, we can stay healthy and strong."

Showing the power of family support: "We know you've had a tough day at work, so we're all going to stay in with you tonight to have a quiet evening at home."

Practicing persistence: "I know it's frustrating and sometime boring to play the same piano piece over and over, but that's what it takes to conquer difficult things."

Teaching the value of working toward a common goal: "I'm sure we would all like to vacation in Europe all summer like the Jones family, but we're saving our money to build an addition onto the house."

Accepting things that can't be changed: "Even though the rain prevents us from having the family reunion in the park, we can still find ways to enjoy being together."

Finding opportunity in adversity: "It's not fair that the factory closed down and we lost that job, but this gives us a chance to rethink what we want to do with our lives."

Practicing winning and losing: "I'm sorry you didn't get that position as class president; you deserved it. But I'm still by your side, and we'll keep moving forward."

What's great about practicing resilient behaviors is that you actually become more resilient with each challenge, regardless of whether or not things go your way. Even if you don't succeed at something, a sense of optimism helps you learn what to do better the next time, and you become stronger from the experience. It's what Southwick calls the "upward spiral of resilience." Has a nice ring to it, doesn't it?

Secrets of Happy Families

Support During Illness

Our daughter was diagnosed with leukemia when she was eleven years old. On the day of diagnosis, my husband, daughter, son, and I sat down and discussed how we would handle the crisis. We agreed that we would stick together and support each other no matter how difficult things got and that we would let the experience bring us together. We took the negative and turned it into a positive by volunteering for different organizations and by appreciating life and each other. We were also blessed to have a supportive "temple family" at the synagogue we belong to.

—Marsha, 41, *married 20 years*

Your General Resiliency Survival Kit

If there's one thing that families have taught me, it's that surviving bad things requires some basic elements that keep you strong and allow you to bounce back. If you'd like to develop resiliency in your family, here are some things to pack inside your survival kit.

A sturdy body and mind. We all need to be just a bit tough to stand up against the stresses of life. Keep your bodies healthy and strong and your minds sharp. Encourage all your family members to stay open to challenging reading and thinking activities (get out the Scrabble board!), enjoy a mentally difficult hobby (dust off that flute or take out the watercolors), and get involved in team and individual sports.

Effective communication skills. Simple changes in how you start discussions and apply good listening skills can help empower family members to feel your support. Apply the communication rules that were addressed in Secret 2 and Secret 6.

Empathy. We each see the world through our own lens—and that's bound to lead to conflict if we aren't open to how others see things. Rather than focus on why your partner, your parents, or your kids are screwing up, take the time to imagine the situation from their point of view. When you do that, and teach your children how to do it, you'll all develop the empathy that supports resiliency.

Lots of love. Research shows that for a couple to thrive, they need to have five positive interactions for every negative one.[8] I'm sure the same dynamic works for all family members. When it comes to love, don't be stingy!

Acceptance. The members of your family are never going to be exact clones of you, so it's important to make an effort to accept their unique personalities and temperaments. When you want your child to be a violinist, but he's tone deaf, or when you are hoping for a ballerina and get a lacrosse player, or when you wish your partner were taller, smarter, or wittier, remember that acceptance is a sign of respect and a tool of the resilient family. This doesn't mean that you should accept socially inappropriate behavior; it just means that you may have to make accommodations for the unique needs and qualities of your family members.

Grace. All family members need to become more thoughtful of others. Some of that comes through cultivating empathy, as mentioned earlier. Further, we all should learn to think of others' needs even before our own.

I saw a family example of this several years ago when my family was invited by Sarah and Bill to celebrate the bar mitzvah of their first child. We knew the drill: go to the party, dance the hora, and then write out a not-so-small check to the thirteen-year-old man. But in this case it wasn't bar mitzvah business as usual. My wife and I were pleasantly surprised to learn about the unusual fate of our money. Unlike most young adults who plan to use their financial gifts for stereo systems or for the future purchase of their cars, Jake decided to buy a new set of drums with the money. Because he already had a drum set worth several hundred dollars, he had the option of selling his drums and using the money to offset the high cost of his new instrument.

Instead, with the encouragement of his parents, Jake chose to donate his drum set to an organization called Mr. Holland's Opus Foundation, an organization that provides instruments for under-privileged children. I asked Sarah why Jake was doing it. "It was a no-brainer for him. Jake wanted to give something to another child that he was already fortunate to own." Three years later, Jake's brother, Sam, did the same thing with his trumpet when he turned thirteen—forgoing the cash buyout at a music store to make sure that a less fortunate person would have the same chance that he did.

When you take this more balanced view of the world, it will help steel all members of your family against adversity in the future.

Realistic expectations. Resilient individuals view mistakes as learning opportunities. Mistakes shouldn't be frowned on—they're part of any endeavor. Help all the members of your family under-stand that they are not expected to be perfect and are loved even when they "mess up," and help them see that they can learn from their errors. Remember to apply this philosophy to yourself as well.

Limits and boundaries. Part of becoming resilient is knowing what falls within bounds and what goes too far. Children need to know what "going too far" looks like—*before* they get there (You cannot cross the street without an adult to help you); so does your mate (No, it's not all right for you to have lunch with that cute sec-retary from accounting) and of course your in-laws (Yes, it's fine to borrow our GPS for your road trip, but please be sure to return it by next weekend). Knowing that there are limits and knowing where they are help keep life in balance, a necessary element in main-taining resiliency.

LIGHTEN UP

Finding that balance brings our happy families to their final secret. As you'll see in the next chapter, after the daily work of applying the secrets of happy families (sticking to values, committing and communicating, giving and taking support, parenting, fighting fair, and bouncing back), they take time to breathe—to laugh and enjoy life and each other.

Happy Families . . .
Breathe

One of the risks of writing a book of "secrets," whether they pertain to having a happy family or building a billion-dollar portfolio or becoming a great golfer, is that I am confronting you with so many tips and pieces of useful advice that there is *no way* you can possibly do all the things I suggest. And if reading such a book feels like an assignment to pile more items on an ever-growing to-do list, then you won't feel better after finishing the final page.

So you're going to like this last chapter because this secret of happy families is all about putting *less* on your list, not more. It's about taking a deep breath, lightening up, and spending mellow time with your family in order to nurture a happier connection with each other.

For example, I was pleasantly surprised when Mary-Jo and her husband, Richard, found time to come to my office for a counseling session, because for both of these accomplished professionals, time is at a premium. They have three children, ages four to ten, and among them they have music classes; T-ball, soccer, and hockey games (depending on the season); dance classes; gymnastics; and tutoring. Moreover, Mary-Jo and Richard both have full-time jobs as physicians. In the midst of all this activity, they sat on my couch looking frazzled and worn out.

"I always feel like I'm behind the eight ball," Mary-Jo began. "We're losing our sense of connection to each other and to the family."

"Yeah," added Richard. "We used to laugh more and have fun. Now it seems like it's all work and no play. I want to go back to the time when we enjoyed being around each other. We thought you might be able to help."

Now I can't fault Mary-Jo and Richard for their hectic lives. They live in an affluent suburb of Providence where, to echo the sentiments of Garrison Keillor, "All the men are strong, all the women are good looking, and all the kids are above average." Like many others in this town, they enroll their children in a vast array of activities because they want what's best for them: they want them to have lots of friends; they want them to be good at sports; they want them to get good grades, get into great colleges, and ultimately have great careers in high-paying jobs that they love. And who can blame these caring parents for making sure they can pay for these things by putting in lots of extra work hours, meeting important contacts, and securing a place of respect and admiration in the community?

So here's the question we all need to answer: When do the enrichment of children and the work and community demands of adults start to interfere with family happiness?

As Mary-Jo and Richard realized, it happens when you're not looking.

Families with real happiness in their lives give generously of themselves to others, but they also know that finding happiness is not a go, go, go scheme. In fact, sometimes it's a stop-and-smell-the-flowers proposition.

Mary-Jo and Richard knew that their family had had enough, and coming to see me was the first step to pulling the plug on the nonstop action. When they returned to my office the following month, they reported back their progress. After a few family meetings, they decided the fate of the kids: one sport per season, one artistic endeavor (dance or instrument) each, and the rest of the time left for family and fun. Mary-Jo explained it like this: "If my little ballerina wants to learn the guitar, that's fine by me. She can pick up my old instrument and teach herself the way I did. I'm not taking her to any more lessons. All the running around had just become too much!"

THE CHRONIC STRESS OF FIGHT OR FLIGHT

Biological science supports what many happy families know. When people slow down their pace, they improve their physical, mental, and emotional health—which has a direct effect on their happiness. But most of us suffer at least occasionally from the opposite of slowing down: we confront the stresses of everyday life by increasing our pace, speeding up, and taking sudden actions that leave us stressed out and exhausted. A brief look at the body's physiology explains why.

The human machine was designed originally for survival under dire circumstances. Imagine, for a moment, what life was like for primitive cave-families living together without any defense against other creatures who might want to inhabit their home for the night. Their days were spent dealing with predators, storms, hostile neighbors, cave-ins, and other moment-to-moment life-or-death experiences. Under such conditions, humans employed instinctive neurological mechanisms, collectively referred to as the fight-or-flight response, to stave off outside dangers.

When confronted with a potentially life-threatening situation, such as our ancestors surely faced on a regular basis, the human body kicks into high gear. The first of a cascade of events happens in the human brain, whose job it is to perceive danger. Once the brain recognizes peril, it releases chemicals that activate small glands located just above the kidneys, called the adrenals. When they are triggered into action, the adrenals release the hormones cortisol and norepinephrine, which travel through the blood to every organ in the human body. And believe me, it is a rush!

As these adrenal hormones race through the body, they prepare it for any impending threat by bracing the body's resources to either fight against the threat or run from it as fast as possible. The blood pressure rises and the heart races, so that oxygen-rich red blood cells can get to all the muscles in the body. The muscles tense, sending slight tremors via the nerve cells. Breathing becomes more shallow as the body quickly removes the "dirty" carbon dioxide and replaces it with fresh oxygen. The liver releases its store of sugar to energize the muscles. Thus strengthened, the human body has a much better chance of escaping the predator or fighting the invading hordes.

All good. But few people I know these days live in caves, and the closest most people come to a bear or lion is in the zoo. Modern life is not filled with the do-or-die moments that affected humans millions or even just thousands of years ago. Our environment has changed, but our bodies haven't. Today's stresses are more low-key but more chronic, and their ever-present status results in some dicey physiological missteps. When individuals consistently maintain high levels of stress, the presence of adrenal hormones begins to wear down the infrastructure of the body. Like a battleship being fired on that never gets repaired because it is always in battle, the body doesn't have time or energy for routine maintenance.

The chronic elevation in blood pressure begins to put strain on the heart and to increase the deposit of dangerous cholesterol plaques in the walls of the blood vessels, increasing the risk of heart disease or stroke. The body's immune system also gets worn down, which not only results in more coughs and colds but also can lead to an inability to ward off long-term inflammatory diseases or even Alzheimer's dementia. Lack of maintenance wears down joints and bones, causing arthritis and osteoporosis. The pernicious effects of the body's elevated blood sugar increase the chances of getting diabetes. Organ by organ, day by day, chronic strain prematurely ages the body and wrecks the quality of life. The resulting unhappiness is also contagious to all members of the family. Soon everyone in the home feels the effects of daily stress.

OVERSCHEDULED LIVES

Where is the source of this chronic stress? It's not a creature hiding in the woods, and it's not a stranger lurking in the rafters waiting to jump us. It is a by-product of our lifestyles and the pressures we put on ourselves to achieve all that we aspire to.

It starts with the busy couple who invest so much time and energy in their careers or volunteer activities that they weaken their connection to each other. And it continues when parents like Mary-Jo and Richard become intent on having their children excel at sports, arts, and academics—all at the same time.

Busy, Busy Kids

I've lived through the trends of intrauterine sound therapeutics, infant Gymboree, and childhood lessons in foreign languages, sign language, and classical music. As children grow, parents' quest to fill their heads with knowledge often turns into a daily marathon. Perhaps idleness is the devil's workshop, but overscheduling children is no ticket to heavenly delights.

Unless you have a full-time nanny (and half a percent of the respondents to the online Happy Family Survey said that they had hired help to take the children to activities), it's a sure bet that filling your children's day with activities means that you too are overworked and overscheduled. One father I know counted fourteen drop-offs and pickups on one Saturday for his three children.

It wouldn't be so bad if the time spent transporting children could even remotely be considered "quality time." But most parents are already running behind for their child's appointment and, by extension, are late picking up the next child. Driving around in traffic with hamburger wrappers and juice boxes being tossed around while dealing with the constant pressure to be somewhere exactly on schedule is not quality time for the kids or the adults. And that kind of daily existence wears kids down until their bodies too begin to suffer the physical signs of chronic stress breakdown.

"But," you may ask, "isn't it good to keep kids busy and active?" Yes, sometimes (an important issue that I address in detail later in this chapter). However, I've noticed that families who describe themselves as happy generally find a way to strike the balance between overscheduled and underscheduled. Although they are involved in community activities, they make sure that their kids have opportunities for spontaneous out-of-doors activities, for daily downtime, and for unhurried play.

Busy, Busy, Busy

As a group, we adults have managed to overschedule almost every aspect of our lives, and unfortunately we are paying a price for our overachievement that is making withdrawals every day from our reserves of family happiness.

Let's identify just a few of the common sources of stress that steal away time from our families until we can't remember what their laughter sounds like.

The stress of too much stuff. We're at a crossroads in American society. We have access to the best medical care we've ever known, educational opportunities for everyone who desires to learn, an information superhighway that can give us anything from the phone number of a neighbor to a map of Timbuktu with the click of a mouse, and a cornucopia of choices in food, clothing, and shelter.

Yet despite the ever-increasing number of global and technological options as a society, we're not any happier. Access to all the resources in the world has set into motion a chain of needs and wants that rival the desires of King Midas. (Remember the Esterling paradox that we spoke about in Chapter 2? Extra things don't make people extra happy.) The more awesome stuff that's out there, the more awesome stuff we want.

This drive to get more and more stuff pulls our time and attention away from our families. Imagine that you could have back all the in-store and online browsing and shopping time you've given away this month and that you could grant that time to your family instead. Just imagine.

The stress of being in touch. When I was growing up, the only way people could reach other people when they weren't home was with a beeper. As I sat through weddings, funerals, baptisms, and bar mitzvahs with my family, we always knew the doctor in the crowd because his or her beeper would disturb the ceremony (there was no vibrate mode back then). The average guy didn't have a beeper. Short of a bona fide crisis (when the police would spread out to find you), when you were away from home, you were out of touch.

It's starting to look as if that wasn't such a bad thing. Now that cell phones are so widely available, more and more family members are "on call" at all times. Valuable family time is traded in when others demand our 24/7 attention for phone calls, text messages, and e-mails. Smack in the middle of a dinner conversation, young Jimmy will say, "Oh I gotta take this call." Or just while you're relating your boss's response to your presentation, your partner will glance down at his or her phone to check who's sending a text message. And even when you're sitting in the park with your family around you, somebody's bound to miss the funny story you're telling because he is talking on a cell phone. (Okay, maybe it wasn't so funny. But he could have been polite and laughed anyway!)

The stress of overinvolvement. Community involvement is a good thing. The value of working together with your family members for the good of a greater cause has been discussed several times in this very book. But being overinvolved in any branch of your community can overwhelm your stress defenses.

A well-known and accomplished businessman was seeing me in therapy hoping to strengthen his marriage. The basics were there: he loved his wife, and she loved him. Although he had been quite successful in work, he had let his home life take a backseat. To his credit, he was making great progress in shifting his priorities; his wife felt loved.

A few months into therapy, though, he had suddenly become very anxious. "I should be happy," he said, announcing that he was nominated to be a board member for a national charitable organization. "It's quite an honor." Although he felt some pressure to accept the position, he wondered whether it might interfere with the time he was now spending with his family. But how could he turn down the coveted opportunity to hold such a prestigious position?

I suggested that he go home and talk to his wife about it. He may not have realized it at the time, but I knew it was not a one-person decision.

When my client returned the next week, he told me that he had decided to decline the position. "Actually," he said, "I'm relieved. My wife and I determined there was just too much good stuff going on at home, and now wouldn't be a good time. We think that once the kids are a little older it might be a more appropriate time."

As my client ultimately realized, if we don't make a conscious effort to relieve the chronic stress that permeates this lifestyle we've become accustomed to, the very foundation of our happy family is bound to crack under the strain.

In your heart of hearts, you know I'm right when I tell you to look for areas where you can cut back to leave time for daily downtime and unhurried and spontaneous family activities. When you let down your guard, you're more prone to being able to find ways that will allow you to exhale in the midst of your busy life.

LEARNING TO BREATHE

There was a time when I made a real effort to master existential thought and Eastern philosophies. For a while in college I walked around with a book on Taoism and tried to absorb its philosophy of "nonaction" as a way to transcend my material self. But then I became a doctor and, more important, a husband and dad. So although I'd like to be able to say that I could handle life by simply letting go, there were some hard realities that didn't allow me to walk around in a state of blissful meditation and inner peace.

Most of my clients are in the same boat; they deal with such real-life demands as paying mortgages or rent, getting kids through college, and, these days, being able to afford gas for the car. So I'd be a fool to advise you simply to "chill" when it comes surviving in Western civilization. For many, that's just not a realistic solution when life in the twenty-first century is inherently hectic. But it's important to recognize that the stress that often accompanies this lifestyle certainly affects the happiness levels of all family members.

If you get creative, I'm sure you can think of lots of ways to give yourself a break. In my experience, there are three dimensions that guide us to calm and relaxation: spiritual, emotional, and physical.

In the next few pages, I'll touch on these aspects of being good to yourself and your family, but remember as I do so that these dimensions overlap considerably. For instance, practicing yoga yields both spiritual and emotional benefits, and praying not only contributes to your religious development but also brings down your blood pressure and heart rate.[1]

The Spiritual Dimension

In Secret 3 we talked about the power of faith and religious belief to help families stay together and overcome adversity. Seeing themselves as part of a higher plan helps set a guiding path for some individuals and families. Moreover, setting aside time each week for the ritual of prayerful reflection within a spiritual community provides a break from daily stresses and allows time to think about things bigger than ourselves. This ritual, along with prayer, has been found to have the power to heal the soul.

In Providence, near Brown University, it isn't at all unusual to see Orthodox Jewish families, recognizable by their traditional garb, walking to synagogue on Friday nights before sundown. In Judaism, Sabbath is the holiest day of the year, and it happens every week! From sunset Friday to sunset Saturday, members of the Orthodox Jewish community use no electricity (that means no laptops either!) and spend the time with their family and their religious community praying or studying. By forcing themselves to literally pull the plug on their hectic lives, these individuals have found a way to re-energize themselves for the week to come.

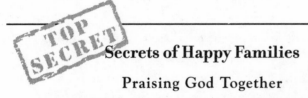

Secrets of Happy Families

Praising God Together

Things have been a bit tough. We had a loss of income for ten months over a two-year span. We have one small child and another one on the way. We have too much debt and not enough salary to cover it. But the most important factor for our happy family is having family worship—praying to and praising God together.

Jeremy, 29, married 4 years

Although some people find peace in this way through strict adherence to religious doctrine, there are also other ways to take a spiritual break from a hectic life schedule. For many people, going for walk in the woods helps them feel part of a grander plan; at the very least, it is relaxing and stress reducing.

In the twenty-four years of my medical practice, I have seen more and more people find calm in the storm of their lives through the spirituality found in yoga. Many people find that yoga makes them feel relaxed and more limber, and there are now studies that show it may actually treat depression and anxiety disorders.[2]

Meditation, breathing exercises, stretching, and awareness of spiritual energy powers (such as chakras) also act as stabilizing forces for people who are at risk of spending all too much time hustling from problem to problem.

SECRETS FROM RESEARCH
Practice Deep Breathing

By learning how to control your breathing, you shift your attention from panic to peacefulness. The technique is simple, although it does take practice.

When you have a moment to yourself, sit in a comfortable, quiet place. Breathe in deeply through your nose, using your diaphragm (the muscle under your rib cage), not your chest, to move the air. The intake of breath should be deliberate, and you should make a point of feeling the fresh, oxygenated, pure air enter your nose. As the intake breath lasts from four to six seconds, visualize the air filling your lungs. Hold for a second or two.

Then, through pursed lips (to make sure the air doesn't rush out too quickly), slowly breathe out, imagining that the exhaled air is expelling impurities and tension from your body. Again, breathe in the fresh, invigorating air, hold for a moment, and follow with a deliberate and slow release of the used air from your lungs.

If you do this breathing exercise for several minutes each day, you will learn to control your breathing during times of stress, and this will reduce the effects of the invasive stress hormones.

Often, doing mindfulness activities together as a family helps synergize the relaxation response. But there are times when the best way to engage in meditation is without your family in tow. Let's face it: it would be the rare family indeed who could take their toddlers to yoga class or bring their teenagers on a meditative walk and be able to see it as a form of relaxation! When it comes to spiritual growth, some of the things that benefit your family most are best done solo. When you come back to the clan calmer and happier, your family benefits from your spiritual strength.

The Emotional Dimension

Emotional rejuvenation is something we all do—often without knowing it. If you're reading this book, you're developing your emotional self. If you periodically sit down to have conversations with your children, your friend, or your partner, then you're developing your emotional self. Any time you take care of yourself in any dimension, even if it's to have a good meal, you are tending to your emotional needs. But beyond this natural form of rejuvenation, we achieve emotional balance when we make a *conscious* effort to control the way we choose to perceive our experiences and actions during our waking hours.

From one moment to the next, your brain is constantly alerting your consciousness about your level of mood and attitude. The remarkable thing about this communication is that you can control the messages your brain sends—if you make a conscious effort to do so.

Let's say, for example, that two girls are sitting at a library table doing some research for their history paper. One sees a mouse scurry quickly right past her feet and then disappear into a small crevice in the corner. Her heart pounds as adrenaline rushes through her body. She jumps up, knocking over her chair, as she struggles to find her voice. The other girl, who didn't notice the mouse, calmly continues her research.

The point is that even though the presence of the mouse was just as real and threatening to the second girl, she didn't have a stress response because she didn't perceive the mouse. That demonstrates the profound role that perception has in dictating your response to stress; it is not an event itself but rather your response to it that's stressful to your body, depending entirely on how you perceive the event.

If we took a balanced view of the things we let upset us each day, we'd realize that more often than not, we get unnecessarily rattled: our reaction is based not on external "reality" but on our perception of it.

Most of us know this instinctively. We ask our children to keep things in perspective when they start the first day of school or have an upcoming bike race or a youth-group trip to a new town. We support our friends, suggesting they not take their blind date so seriously or not worry that their house hasn't sold the first week it is on the market. We offer this advice to our loved ones because we can clearly see when they are blowing things out of proportion. We'd be wise to take our own advice.

SECRETS FROM RESEARCH
It's the Attitude

I am more and more convinced that our happiness or our unhappiness depends far more on the way we meet the events of life than on the nature of those events themselves.
—*Karl Wilhelm von Humboldt (1767–1835), German statesman*

The Physical Dimension

It's probably not news for anyone who has carefully examined the human form: the brain is attached to the rest of the body. What you can't see from the outside, though, is that through the circulatory, nervous, and endocrine systems, the body and brain constantly send messages back and forth, something along these lines:

BRAIN: "How you doin'?"

BODY: "How *you* doin'?" and so on.

When an individual is physically active, the interchange goes like this:

BODY: "I love how these stretching exercises are limbering up my muscles, joints, and tendons."

BRAIN: "Hey—I'm not getting any tension-filled messages right now. I can relax and hold back on those stress hormones; instead, I think I'll release some of these 'feel good' endorphins."

This connection between the body's physical health and the brain's perception of health is as vital as the spiritual and emotional dimensions in reducing the stress that interferes with living a joyous and fulfilling life.

I acknowledge that finding the right balance between good nutrition, good medical care, and physical activity while nurturing the day-to-day needs of everyone in the family is sometimes a challenge. So let's focus here on one of the basics that has a major influence on one's health: physical inactivity and overeating.

Hey, we all have to eat, right? So how can turning down a second donut possibly affect my health and the happiness of my family? Well, if that second donut begins to show on a belly that hangs over your belt, you're joining a large group of people who put their health, and therefore their family's happiness, at risk. The 2003–2004 National Health and Nutrition Examination Survey reports that about 66 percent of U.S. adults are either overweight or obese.[3] The surgeon general's report points out that three hundred thousand individuals die each year from obesity-related illness and that associated medical costs exceed $117 billion.[4] That's a lot of families affected by poor physical health.

The family can be one of the most influential forces in helping individuals stay healthy. We can help our children from day one by practicing, modeling, and teaching good eating habits and by cautioning against drug, alcohol, and cigarette use. And we have an especially strong role to play in encouraging all our family members to be more physically active.

Secrets of Happy Families

Staying Involved

The secret of our happy family is being involved in our children's lives. We coach their baseball teams and go camping year round. We ride quads, motorcycles, wakeboard and go boating together. We are always trying new activities to broaden our kids' interests and keep them in physical shape. Also, it keeps them from getting bored, and there's always something to talk about at dinner. Not one of our kids has done drugs, run away, or become a teenage mother. Thank God.

Tracey, 38, cohabiting with boyfriend, household of six children

---

Protecting the physical health of all family members should be ingrained in your family psyche. In Secret 1, we talked about the importance of shared values; well, here we find the same guiding principle. If you teach your family to value good food and exercise, these will become a part of your family identity. This is particularly important when there are children in the home.

In one of the largest studies of its kind, from 2000 until 2006, researchers (funded by the National Institute of Child Health and Human Development) assessed physical movement by attaching special gadgets to one thousand American children. They found that the amount of activity time fell from about three hours a day at age nine to less than an hour a day by age fifteen. During the week, less than one-third of the teens got the recommended amount of physical activity, and they did even less exercise during the weekend.[5] The researchers suggest that the rise in computer use and virtual gaming has stolen away physicality from our youth. I agree.

Too many kids tend to glue themselves to steel and glass devices that isolate them from others. Children today believe that TV,

SECRETS FROM RESEARCH
Stop the Obsession

Some electronic devices can increase stress levels in kids. One nurse I worked with, John, described his eleven-year-old daughter who was devastated, *devastated*, when her cousin stole her password, went online, and "sold" all the weapons and treasures she had earned playing *Warcraft*. So bereft was she that she cried for hours, and repeatedly placed threatening and angry phone calls to her cousins, aunt, and uncle. Now, truly, I do understand how, after spending hundreds of hours earning those virtual treasures, this was an awful thing for her cousin to have done. But both John and I agreed that this had become more than a game; it had become an obsession. As far as John was concerned, that was the last time his daughter would ever play that game.

video games, the Internet, and iPods are all must-have survival tools. But like anything else, too much of a good thing can turn bad when it steals precious time away from other activities that build health and family togetherness.

All our kids have electronic toys, so how can we tell if those gadgets are too severely limiting their physical activity? Easy. Do your children (or you, for that matter) engage in any unscheduled and spontaneous out-of-doors activities? One of my children's grade school teachers gave her students the homework assignment to go out and play for a half hour each day after school. Maybe we should all give that assignment to our children—from toddlerhood through the teens. If they don't have time to do that, they're overscheduled. If they hate to do that, they probably need some help getting unplugged from their electronic playmates.

The health—and happiness—of your family require that every member of the family take time each day to care for himself or

SECRETS FROM RESEARCH
A Decline in Free Time for Kids

A report based on national time diary surveys conducted in 1981 and 1997 notes a major decline in the free time of children ages three to twelve.[6] The findings show

- A twelve-hour-per-week decline in overall free time for children

- A decrease of three hours per week in playtime

- A 50 percent decrease in unstructured outdoor activities (including such activities as walking, hiking, or camping)

Isn't it time we do something within our families to change this trend?

herself physically. That means doing something (preferably together) that gets you up and moving! Tell your brain to hold off on those stress hormones and send out the message to your entire body that life is good.

FAMILY TIME

The online Happy Family Survey taught me a lot about the things that a variety of people believe contribute to family happiness. In ranking given factors, resiliency came out on top (thus earning itself an entire chapter in Secret 7). In a very close second, respondents endorsed doing a lot of activities as a family. In fact, although this wasn't always selected as first choice, it made the top three (of six) choices more often than any other factor—76 percent of folks felt that doing things together as a family mattered.

Secrets of Happy Families

Time Is the Most Important Thing

This is the second marriage for both my husband and me. He has two children from his first marriage, and we have one child together. On your survey, I marked "Doing lots of activities" as being important, but they don't need to be big activities. It can be something as small as eating family dinners. Time to me is the most important thing you can give each other, as a spouse, mother, father, or sibling. When we do things as a family, it creates time to communicate. Consequently, we have very open and honest communication in our household, and that is really important to all of us.

—Jodi, 36, *married 9 years*

When you spend time with your family, you give a clear message that you care about them and that being with them brings you joy. Yeah, I know, spending the night playing poker with your buddies or hiding away in your bedroom and reading a novel brings you joy also, and, trust me, you'll have plenty of time for those things too. But families who spend time with each other are happier. In fact, the simple act of eating meals together has been proven to reduce the risk of teenage sex, alcohol or drug use, school fights or suspensions, or thoughts of suicide.[7] That's a powerful antidote for many of the forces that pull families apart.

The time together doesn't have to be with the whole family, every time, en masse. Juan, age forty and married for thirteen years, wrote on the Happy Family Survey, "The most important factor for happiness is spending time with my family and making them a priority. I have date night with my wife once a week and special days with my son and daughter once a week each." Now *that's* what I'm talking about!

Secrets of Happy Families

No Electronic Games for Us

Hands-on is the only way to live! Turning off the TV and restricting the video games, going outside, and playing games in the fresh air—even activities as simple as a family walk matter. Playing board games inside and being creative is of the essence in family life. My sister, Lana, and I have been playing Scrabble for thirty-eight years together, and we pass on the tradition with our families. When my nephews and nieces visit me, they go straight to the printer, grab a piece of paper, and draw me a picture of the upcoming holiday or something special. I have the infamous "Aunt Barbara Creative Wall" where I am proud of all their drawings and creations. I bake cakes with my niece, or I play card games with my nephew. There are so many better things to do than sit passively in front of a TV.

—*Barbara, 49, married 20 years*

My eighteen-year-old son tried to teach me how to play NCAA Football on his Playstation 3, and I was abysmal at it. We also play racquetball together—and I'm abysmal at that too! But both activities give us priceless time together. These moments have become part of the structure that strengthens our connection and allow us to keep building one experience on top of another. This is the stuff of a solid family.

I could spend several pages listing all the fun things you could do with your family, from flying kites to producing your own movie for the grandparents. The important thing is that you find some activity that means something to you that you can share with other members of your family, and also that you stay open to activities that they may want to share with you.

Today that activity may be as simple as showing your young daughter and son how to make Jell-O, while they show you how to weave a friendship bracelet or kick a soccer ball. Down the road, as your family grows, you may be blessed with the opportunity to show them how to heal their babies' diaper rashes while they show you how best to invest your IRA payouts.

That's the wonderful thing about happy families. They thrive year after year, changing together through each stage of life. Which brings us, dear reader, to the next and final message of this book: happy families are not static—they evolve.

Epilogue

Happy Families . . .
Evolve

For hours upon hours over the last months, my wife would find my nose buried in my MacBook and would wonder what was holding my interest so intently. Many times she'd have to say "dinner's ready" three times before I heard.

What drew my attention away from her and toward my computer screen? It was the extraordinary insights, comments, and stories of the individuals who contributed to my online Happy Family Survey.

Professionally, I have worked for almost twenty-five years helping individuals and families with mental health problems. In that time, I have learned that when it comes to family secrets, unless you ask, you don't find out. By asking specifically how people look at their families and what elements make for happy families, I came away learning more than I thought possible.

There were times when I was moved to tears over the stories that people shared with me—and I'm not the kind of guy who cries easily. I didn't cry because of people's hardships, although there were many people who had endured some real tough going. My eyes welled up as I read story after story of how people triumphed over their misfortunes and maintained hope, strength, and a vision for the future.

People shared their accounts of separation or divorce; they talked about this change in their family status as an opportunity to form stronger bonds with their own parents, to redefine themselves as a single parent, or to clear the slate to start a new family. People told of losing their houses and how they embraced the task of rebuilding from scratch. The spoke of picking up the pieces after losing jobs and losing fortunes. And, most profoundly, some told of their slow recovery after losing beloved parents, spouses, or children.

Not a single one of the respondents suggested that mending the wounds of family hurt was easy; each recognized the challenges involved when the expected patterns of family life evolved and shifted in new directions. But these folks all had a special kind of toughness, one that combined the grit to hang in there when things weren't going well with the passionate sense of human connection that bound them to the other members of their families.

What kept these people going? How did they keep their heads above water? A high school teacher would probably like us to believe that it was their good education. A physician would suggest that it was their good health. A priest or rabbi might give credit to a person's relationship with God. I am sure all these things helped. But the one theme that resonated strongest with me was how the family, yes, the family itself, propelled individuals through hardships as devastating as Hurricane Katrina or 9/11, through bank foreclosures and tragic illnesses, and left them standing, bruised but not broken, with the passion to carry on another day. Their stories showed me in vivid true-life detail that it's the brothers, sisters, parents, partners, and children who all weave together to form our most valuable web of support in times of change.

All this talk of rising above the elements can make it sound as if this family stuff is all work and no play, but that's not at all the picture painted by these families. They made it clear that part of being a happy family was learning to evolve as life changed around them, always holding tight to their love for each other—to the pure pleasure of being in each other's company. Getting together for family reunions, e-mailing each other pictures of the kids (or the vacation or the dog), or spending evenings playing Yahtzee in the parlor were all small but important things that these families did to improve their bond and secure that very important web of support.

This willingness to adapt and change, while still making time for fun, illustrated for me an important underlying message of this book: the secrets shared by all these families are not about absolutes. They do not offer insights that are static, unchangeable, and finite. Indeed, as we discussed in the first two chapters of this book, the very words *family* and *happiness* can't easily be defined to apply neatly to everyone. Whatever makes a family a happy, united, and loving gang today may not do so tomorrow. The kids grow up, our relationship with our mate changes, our interests and passions evolve. That's life. While we change and life around us changes, our relationship with each member of our family will also change, and the things that bring us happiness will change as well.

None of this is a problem if we can accept and embrace these changes and hold on to that one constant that is the core of every family secret shared in this book. It is best expressed in the words of Norman MacEwan (1881–1953), air vice marshal of the Royal Air Force, who once said, "Happiness is not so much in having as sharing. We make a living by what we get, but we make a life by what we give."

My hope is that by spending time reading this book and learning how all the individuals within a family give happiness to each other, you'll be inspired to make a conscious effort to give happiness to everyone in your family, and will then in turn enjoy the happiness they give back to you for the rest of your life.

As your family changes and evolves over the years, I am hoping that you and those who have participated in my online survey will keep me informed through my Web site DrScott.com about the things that fill you with joy. Call me a sentimentalist or call me a concerned physician, but if your family's happy, then I'm happy!

Appendix

Aggregate Results of the Happy Family Survey

The information that follows represents the answers collected from participants in an (optionally) anonymous online survey from February 1, 2008, until December 5, 2008. The survey included demographic (age, nationality, and so on), multiple-choice, and narrative questions. When multiple-choice questions were asked (as in the sections on values or roles), the computer program automatically altered the order of the possible answers in order to avoid selection bias. Only the answers to demographic or multiple-choice questions are included in this Appendix. Some individuals did not answer all of the questions, so total responses may vary across different parts of the survey.

Demographic Information

Total completing the Happy Family Survey: 1,266
Thirty-four different countries represented, primarily the United States

Sex:
  314 male
  829 female
Age (years):
  Average (mean): 41
  Mode: 42
  Median: 44
  Range: 14–76

Average number of people in household: 3.74
Marital status:
  Married or "common law" married: 1,049
  Average length of marriage: 16.5 years

WHAT MAKES A FAMILY?

1. Who currently comprises your family?

	Response Percentage	Response Count
Who are the adults in your family?		
Spouse (opposite sex)	81.4%	1,015
Unmarried companion (opposite sex)	8.5%	106
Same-sex "romantic" companion or spouse	1.7%	21
Who are the children in your family?		
Biological child(ren) of current spouse/companion	56.3%	702
Stepchild(ren)	20.9%	261
Foster child(ren)	0.7%	9
Who are "others" in your family?		
Parent(s) or other family member(s)	9.6%	120
Pet(s)	39.5%	493
Other	8.7%	108
answered question		1,247

2. How happy are you with your current family life?

	Response Percentage	Response Count
Extremely happy	30.2%	381
Moderately happy	28.0%	353
Somewhat happy	13.3%	167
Neutral	5.6%	70
Somewhat unhappy	6.0%	75
Moderately unhappy	3.3%	41
Extremely unhappy	2.1%	27
	answered question	1,260

3. How happy do you think your family members are with their family life?

	Response Percentage	Response Count
Extremely happy	27.1%	338
Moderately happy	41.8%	521
Somewhat happy	16.3%	203
Neutral	4.3%	54
Somewhat unhappy	6.3%	79
Moderately unhappy	2.4%	30
Extremely unhappy	1.8%	22
	answered question	1,247

4. Of the factors listed, how important is each of these for making a happy family?

	Most Important	Second Most Important	Third Most Important	Fourth Most Important	Fifth Most Important	Least Important	Response Count
Resiliency (ability to bounce back from bad experiences)	29.1% (343)	23.0% (271)	19.4% (228)	16.0% (189)	9.8% (115)	2.7% (32)	1,178
Doing a lot of activities as a family	26.1% (306)	26.9% (316)	23.3% (274)	16.0% (188)	6.3% (74)	1.4% (16)	1,174
Having children grow up with both biological parents	26.2% (304)	19.6% (228)	14.1% (164)	14.2% (165)	14.5% (169)	11.4% (132)	1,162
Attending religious services regularly	15.8% (186)	11.6% (137)	9.5% (112)	12.8% (150)	18.5% (218)	31.7% (373)	1,176
Agreeing about money	6.7% (79)	17.5% (206)	28.4% (333)	24.5% (288)	16.8% (197)	6.0% (71)	1,174
Living within an hour's distance from children's grandparents	0.7% (8)	2.8% (33)	6.2% (73)	14.9% (175)	30.7% (359)	44.7% (523)	1,171

answered question 1,238

5. Below are listed many "Values" that people hold. Of those listed, please indicate which you believe are the top three values held by your family.

	Response Count	Most Important	Second Most Important	Third Most Important
Personal and emotional growth	595	240	208	147
Comfort at home	461	192	153	116
Health	419	162	155	102
Spiritual fulfillment	403	260	68	75
Financial security	375	75	126	174
Learning	224	45	98	81
Making a contribution to society	218	37	72	109
Work/employment	198	40	85	73
Friends	170	18	74	78
Generosity	146	33	47	66

Formal education	125	18	61	46
Serenity	92	25	26	41
Other	59	42	9	8
Diversity	33	7	6	20
Travel	33	2	7	24
Protecting family secrets	26	9	7	10
Justice	26	7	5	14
Personal appearance	19	2	6	11
Material possessions	15	2	4	9
Fame	9	2	1	6
Elegance	6	1	2	3

answered question 1,231

6. Who works outside of your home? (check all that apply)

	Response Percentage	Response Count
The man in the house does full-time work one job	71.0%	882
The woman in the house does full-time work one job	45.4%	564
The woman in the house works part time only	19.2%	239
The man in the house does full-time work **and** does part-time work	15.6%	194
The woman in the house chooses not to work outside the home	13.7%	170
Children who live at home work	12.1%	151
The woman in the house does full-time work **and** does part-time work	8.4%	104

The man in the house works part time only	▪	4.3%	53
The adult(s) in the home is (are) retired	▪	3.8%	47
The adult(s) in the home is (are) unemployed and looking for work	▪	3.1%	38
No adult man lives in the house	▪	3.1%	38
The man in the house chooses not to work outside the house	▪	1.4%	17
No adult woman lives in the house	▪	1.0%	13

answered question   1,243

7. How are roles divided in your household? (Check all that apply)

	Adult Male	Adult Female	Children	Hired Help	Doesn't Apply	Response Count
Lawn care	67.3% (830)	25.2% (311)	13.8% (170)	12.9% (159)	12.2% (150)	1,233
Laundry	42.7% (530)	91.1% (1,131)	19.6% (243)	2.7% (33)	0.6% (7)	1,242
Taking children to appointments	36.3% (444)	74.1% (905)	3.3% (40)	0.5% (6)	20.5% (251)	1,222
Cooking meals	49.2% (611)	90.7% (1,127)	11.6% (144)	1.0% (12)	0.5% (6)	1,242
Vacuuming	42.0% (520)	74.7% (925)	23.7% (293)	10.7% (132)	2.4% (30)	1,238

Doing dishes	56.8% (706)	85.9% (1,069)	28.5% (354)	1.8% (23)	0.7% (9)	1,244
Paying bills	54.0% (673)	72.3% (901)	1.5% (19)	0.1% (1)	0.4% (5)	1,247
Initiating sex	83.2% (1,013)	62.0% (755)	0.0% (0)	0.0% (0)	7.8% (95)	1,214
Calling/writing to family and friends	44.4% (547)	93.2% (1,148)	14.8% (182)	0.0% (0)	2.7% (33)	1,232
Fixing broken household items	84.2% (1,044)	35.7% (443)	5.7% (71)	9.8% (121)	0.8% (10)	1,240
Buying relationship books	21.6% (261)	64.9% (783)	0.4% (5)	0.0% (0)	25.2% (304)	1,206

answered question 1,253

8. Which of the following statements best reflects your beliefs about methods of discipline?

	Response Percentage	Response Count
Children should strictly follow rules and expectations set up by parents.	22.5%	273
Children should be encouraged to question authority to promote independent thinking, even if it means they challenge their parents.	38.3%	464
Neither of the above.	40.6%	493
answered question		1,213

Notes

Introduction

1. U.S. Census Bureau. "Living Arrangements of Children." *2004 Household Economic Studies* (P70-114), Feb. 2008. www.census.gov/prod/2008pubs/p70-114.pdf.

Chapter 1: What Is a Family?

1. "Family." *Webster's Third New International Dictionary of the English Language Unabridged.* Springfield, Mass.: Merriam-Webster, 2002.

2. Hughes, Rachael. "Family Versus Familia, Historical Definitions of the Family." Suite 101, July 1, 2000. www.suite101.com/article.cfm/history_european_family/41658.

3. "Family." Encyclopædia Britannica Online, 2008. www.britannica.com/EBchecked/topic/201237/family.

4. Henderson, Bruce. *True North: Perry, Cook, and the Race to the Pole.* New York: Norton, 2005.

Chapter 2: What Is Happiness?

1. McGowan, Kathleen. "The Pleasure Paradox." *Psychology Today,* Jan.-Feb. 2008. www.psychologytoday.com/articles/pto-20050119-000005.html.

2. Seligman, Martin. *Authentic Happiness: Using the New Positive Psychology to Realize Your Potential for Lasting Fulfillment.* New York: Free Press, 2004.

3. Dunn, Elizabeth W., Aknin, Lara B., and Norton, Michael I. "Spending Money on Others Promotes Happiness." *Science*, Mar. 21, 2008, *319*, 1687–1688.

4. Gilbert, Daniel. *Stumbling on Happiness*. New York: Knopf, 2006.

5. Leonhardt, David. "Maybe Money Does Buy Happiness After All." *New York Times*, Apr. 16, 2008. www.nytimes.com/2008/04/16/business/16leonhardt.html?scp=6&sq=happiness%20and%20income&st=cse.

6. Foltz-Gray, Dorothy. "What Makes Us Happy?" Depression Forums, Mar. 28, 2008. www.depressionforums.org/articles/1009/1/What-Makes-Us-Happy/Page1.html.

7. Mill, John Stuart. *The Autobiography of John Stuart Mill*. New York: Cosimo Classics, 2007.

Secret 1: Happy Families Stick Together

1. Orecklin, Michele. "Stress and the Superdad." *Time*, Aug. 16, 2004, pp. 38–39.

2. Feynman, Richard, and Leighton, Ralph. *Surely You're Joking, Mr. Feynman!* New York: Norton, 1997.

3. Lundberg, Rose. "The Effects of Sons and Daughters on Men's Labor Supply and Wages." *Review of Economics and Statistics*, 2002, 84(2), 251–268.

Secret 2: Happy Families Commit and Communicate

1. Waite, Linda, and Gallagher, Maggie. *The Case for Marriage: Why Married People Are Happier, Healthier and Better Off Financially*. New York: Broadway Books, 2001.

2. Shrider, Marylee. "Not All of Our Youth Find Marriage Outdated." *Bakersfield Californian*, Jan. 4, 2008. www.bakersfield.com/opinion/columnists/marylee_shrider/story/326562.html.

3. U.S. Census Bureau. "Number, Timing and Duration of Marriages and Divorces: 2001 Household." *Economic Studies* (P70-97), Feb. 2005. www.census.gov/prod/2005pubs/p70-97.pdf.

4. Parker-Pope, Tara. "Reinventing Date Night for Long-Married Couples." *New York Times*, Feb. 12, 2008, p. F5.

5. Kaplan, Robert M., and Kronick, Richard G. "Marital Status and Longevity in the United States Population." *Journal of Epidemiology and Community Health*, 2006, 60, 760–765.

6. Oliwenstein, Lor. "Marry Me." *Time*, Jan. 28, 2008, p. 76.

7. Oliwenstein, 2008.

8. Gottman, John M., and DeClaire, Joan. *The Relationship Cure: A 5 Step Guide to Strengthening Your Marriage, Family, and Friendships*. New York: Three Rivers Press, 2002.

9. Sullivan, Julie. "Same-Sex Couples Tend to Go Along, Get Along." *Oregonian*, Apr. 10, 2008.

10. Farrell, Waverly, and Doolittle, Vicki. "Accidental Prophets." Paper presented at the 12th annual conference of the Coalition for Marriage, Family and Couples Education, San Francisco, July 4, 2008.

Secret 3: Happy Families Lean

1. Mahoney, David, and Restak, Richard. *The Longevity Strategy: How to Live to 100 Using the Brain-Body Connection*. Hoboken, N.J.: Wiley, 1999, p. 84.

2. Putnam, Robert. *Bowling Alone: The Collapse and Revival of American Community*. New York: Simon & Schuster, 2001, p. 327.

3. Putnam, 2001.

4. Hutter, Mark. *The Changing Family*. (3rd ed.) Boston: Allyn & Bacon, 1998.

Secret 4: Happy Families Teach to and Learn from Children

1. Paul, Pamela. *Parenting, Inc.* New York: Times Books, 2008.

2. Committee on Public Education, American Academy of Pediatrics. "Children, Adolescents, and Television." *Pediatrics*, Feb. 2001, 107(2), 423–426.

3. Anderson, Daniel, and Pempek, Tiffany. "Television and Very Young Children." *American Behavioral Scientist*, Jan. 2005, 48(5), 505–552.

4. Wood, Mark D., Read, Jennifer P., Mitchell, Roger E., and Brand, Nancy H. "Do Parents Still Matter? Parent and Peer Influences on Alcohol Involvement Among Recent High School Graduates." *Psychology of Addictive Behavior*, 2004, 18(1), 19–30.

5. Moore, Kristin A., and others. "Parent-Teen Relationships and Interactions: Far More Positive Than Not." *Child Trends Research Brief* (Pub. no. 2004-25). Washington, D.C.: Child Trends, Dec. 2004. www.childtrends.org/Files/Parent_TeenRB.pdf.

6. Mogel, Wendy. *The Blessing of the Skinned Knee*. New York: Penguin Books, 2001, p. 32.

7. Marano, Hara. *A Nation of Wimps*. New York: Broadway Books, 2008.

8. University of Oxford. "Grandma and Grandpa Are Good for Children." *ScienceDaily*, June 7, 2008. www.sciencedaily.com–/releases/2008/06/080605091358.htm.

9. Gurian, Michael, and Stevens, Kathy. *The Minds of Boys: Saving Our Sons from Falling Behind in School and Life*. San Francisco: Jossey-Bass, 2007.

10. Gottman, John M., and Katz, Lynn Fainsilber. "Effects of Marital Discord on Young Children's Peer Interactions and Health." *Developmental Psychology*, 1989, 25(3), 373–381.

Secret 5: Happy Families Blend

1. Stanley, Scott M. *The Power of Commitment: A Guide to Active, Lifelong Love*. San Francisco: Jossey-Bass, 2005.

2. Newman, David M., and Grauerholz, Elizabeth. *Sociology of Families*. (2nd ed.) Thousand Oaks, Calif.: Pine Forge Press, 2002.

3. U.S. Census Bureau. "Living Arrangements of Children." *2004 Household Economic Studies* (P70-114), Feb. 2008. www.census.gov/prod/2008pubs/p70-114.pdf.

4. Newman and Grauerholz, 2002.

5. Einstein, Elizabeth. "The Stepfamily Journey: Not for Wimps." Paper presented at the 12th annual conference of the Coalition for Marriage, Family and Couples Education, San Francisco, July 3, 2008.

6. U.S. Census Bureau. "Number, Timing and Duration of Marriages and Divorces: 2001 Household." *Economic Studies* (P70-97), Feb. 2005. www.census.gov/prod/2005pubs/p70-97.pdf.

7. "U.S. Divorce Statistics." *Divorce Magazine*, 2008. www.divorcemag.com/statistics/statsUS.shtml.

8. Popkin, Michael, and Einstein, Elizabeth. "Active Parenting in Stepfamilies." Paper presented at the 12th annual conference of the Coalition for Marriage, Family and Couples Education, San Francisco, July 3, 2008.

Secret 6: Happy Families Handle Conflict

1. Gottman, John M., and Silver, Nan. *The Seven Principles for Making Marriage Work*. New York: Crown, 1999.

2. Eaker, Elaine D., and others. "Marital Status, Marital Strain, and Risk of Coronary Heart Disease or Total Mortality: The Framingham Offspring Study." *Psychosomatic Medicine*, July 18, 2007, 69, 509–513.

3. Gottman, John M., and others. "Correlates of Gay and Lesbian Couples' Relationship Satisfaction and Relationship Dissolution." *Journal of Homosexuality*, 2003, 45(1), 23–43.

4. Gottman and Silver, 1999.

5. Gottman and Silver, 1999.

6. Gottman and Silver, 1999.

7. Eaker and others, 2007.

Secret 7: Happy Families Bounce

1. Southwick, Steven. "Psychosocial and Biological Factors Associated with Resilience to Stress." *Yale Psychiatry*, Summer 2007, 10, 6–8.

2. Caspi, Avshalom, and others. "Influence of Life Stress on Depression: Moderation by a Polymorphism in the 5-HTT Gene." *Science*, July 18, 2003, 9, 302–386.

3. Hughes, Debra. "Do Genetics and Childhood Combine to Pose Risk for Adult PTSD?" *Neuropsychiatry Review*, Apr. 2008, 9, 1.

4. Werner, Emmy, and Smith, Ruth S. *Overcoming the Odds: High Risk Children from Birth to Adulthood*. New York: Cornell University Press, 1992.

5. Southwick, 2007.

6. McCubbin, Hamilton I., and others. "Families Under Stress: What Makes Them Resilient." Article based on the 1997 American Association of Family and Consumer Sciences Commemorative Lecture, Washington, D.C., June 22, 1997. www.cyfernet.org/research/resilient.html.

7. Robinson, Jean. "What Makes Families Resilient?" *TSBVI*, Spring 1999. Texas School for the Blind and Visually Impaired. www.tsbvi.edu/Outreach/seehear/spring99/resilient.htm.

8. Gottman, and Silver, 1999.

Secret 8: Happy Families Breathe

1. Benson, Herbert. *Beyond the Relaxation Response*. New York: Times Books, 1984.

2. Streeter, Chris C., and others. "Yoga Asana Sessions Increase Brain GABA Levels: A Pilot Study." *Journal of Alternative and Complementary Medicine*, 2007, 13(4), 419–426.

3. National Center for Health Statistics. "Prevalence of Overweight and Obesity Among Adults: United States, 2003–2004," Apr. 2006. www.cdc.gov/nchs/products/pubs/pubd/hestats/overweight/overwght_adult_03.htm.

4. U.S. Department of Health and Human Services. "Overweight and Obesity: At a Glance," Jan. 2007. www.surgeongeneral.gov/topics/obesity/calltoaction/fact_glance.htm.

5. Nader, Philip R., and others. "Moderate-to-Vigorous Physical Activity from Ages 9 to 15 Years." *Journal of the American Medical Association*, 2008, 300(3), 295–305.

6. Doherty, William. "Overscheduled Kids, Underconnected Families: The Research Evidence." http://www.extension.umn.edu/parenteducation/research.pdf. Hofferth, Sandra L. "How American Children Spend Their Time." *Journal of Marriage and the Family,* 2001, *63,* 295–308.

7. National Center on Addiction and Substance Abuse. "Family Day—A Day to Eat Dinner with Your Children," Sept. 25, 2004. www.casafamilyday.org.

About the Authors

Scott Haltzman, M.D., is a clinical assistant professor of psychiatry and human behavior at the Warren Alpert Medical School of Brown University, and medical director of NRI Community Services in Rhode Island. He is the author of *The Secrets of Happily Married Men* and *The Secrets of Happily Married Women*. He serves as a member of the "Love Network" for *Redbook*. His insights on families and relationships have led to appearances on the *Today Show, 20/20, Good Morning America*, and features in *Time* magazine, the *New York Times*, the *Washington Post*, and other publications. You can reach him at DrHaltzman@happilymarriedwomen.com.

Theresa Foy DiGeronimo, M.Ed., is the author of fifty-eight books in the fields of parenting, education, and medicine. She is the co-author of *Raising Baby Green, College of the Overwhelmed, Launching Our Black Children for Success*, and *How to Talk to Your Adult Children About Really Important Things*, as well as Scott Haltzman's two previous books, *The Secrets of Happily Married Men* and *The Secrets of Happily Married Women*, all from Jossey-Bass. She is an adjunct professor of English at William Paterson University of New Jersey and also a high school teacher in her hometown of Hawthorne, New Jersey, where she lives with her husband, three children, and a dog named Snowball.

Index

Page references followed by *t* indicate a table.